YOU,
ME &
MARK

Also by Adrian Plass

Silver Birches: A Novel

The Sacred Diary of Adrian Plass, Aged 37¾

*The Sacred Diary of Adrian Plass,
Christian Speaker, Aged 45¾*

*And Jesus Will Be Born: A Collection of Christmas Poems,
Stories and Reflections*

The Best in Plass

*The Sacred Diaries: Encounters with Leonard Thynn and
Andromeda Veal*

You, Me and Mark

Growing Up, Following Jesus

YOU, ME & MARK

A Non-Theologian's Encounter

with the Gospel of Mark

Previously published as *Never Mind the Reversing Ducks*

INTERNATIONALLY BESTSELLING AUTHOR

ADRIAN PLASS

ZONDERVAN®

ZONDERVAN.com/
AUTHORTRACKER
follow your favorite authors

ZONDERVAN

You, Me, and Mark
Copyright © 2002 by Adrian Plass

Previously Published as *Never Mind the Reversing Ducks*

Requests for information should be addressed to:

Zondervan, *Grand Rapids, Michigan* 49530

Adrian Plass asserts the moral right to be identified as the author of this work.

ISBN 978-0-310-29340-8

Interior design by Beth Shagene

Printed in the United States of America

09 10 11 12 13 14 15 • 22 21 20 19 18 17 16 15 14 13 12 11 10 9 8 7 6 5 4 3 2 1

This book is dedicated to Paul Taphouse,
musician, poet and best of friends.

Introduction

SOME YEARS AGO I WROTE A SPOOF ANGLICAN SERMON which I have since performed on hundreds – perhaps even thousands of occasions. In one sense it is a little dated. Broadly speaking the Anglican church, of which I am a puzzled but proud member, has changed for the better. A lot of the dear but deadly old stereotypes are much less evident, and there really does seem to be an increased desire among church members for human and spiritual reality. Having said that, you mustn't worry. We Anglicans are never going to completely run out of things for everyone else to laugh at. Here is an extract from my spoof sermon.

> Good evening, tonight I'd like to share with you a portion of scripture that has always meant a tremendous amount to me. It comes from what I like to call the gynecological letter, Paul's epistle to the Fallopians. In it we are told about one group of people that, and I quote, 'they went down'. They didn't go up, as I think many of us might have done in their place, they went down. They descended. They started at the top and they ended at the bottom. If you like they reversed the direction of their perpendicular motion. One could almost say that they changed their altitude. They went down.
>
> And it's interesting to note that the original Greek word used here has a very strong sense of waterfowl flying backwards. So, what the writer is actually saying is that they went down like *reversing ducks*, and so, of course, should we ...

So there it is. You will find no backward-flying water fowl in general, or reversing ducks in particular anywhere in these pages. There are many theologians and students of the Bible writing fine books about the gospels, but I am not one of them.

What I hope you will find in this book is an honest attempt to respond to the life and words of Jesus as most of us encounter them when we read the New Testament. I do not claim to have all or most of the answers, in fact you will find that my response to some passages is inconclusive and uncertain. I make no apology for that. There is too much pretending in the church as it is. But you will also find that there are times when I get quite carried away by the excitement of reading about the things that Jesus said and did. I make no apology for that either.

I chose Mark's gospel because it seems to me the most vivid and dramatic of the four, and because many people think it was the first to be written (the fact that it was the shortest might have had a little bit to do with it as well). I gather that this gospel was probably intended for Christians in Rome, a place where believers suffered a great deal of persecution. This would make sense, as there is much about the inevitability of suffering, and a lot of encouragement for those who are going through hard times. In Jesus we meet a dynamic, hardworking, passionate member of the human race, a man, but a man who was also God. Stronger than all the powers of nature, he was nevertheless willing to become a servant so that people like you and I can be rescued from the worst of disasters.

I have had a passion for Jesus for many years. It has been such a privilege to be allowed to write this book, and the experience has been very valuable for me. I pray that it will also be of use to you as you join me. Finally, as always, I do hope you have a jolly good read.

The Gospel According to St Mark

The Beginning

1 : 1

The beginning of the good news of Jesus Christ,
the Son of God.

I THINK I MUST HAVE BEEN A RATHER ODD CHILD. AS A VERY
small boy I spent quite a lot of my time trying to imagine
what it would be like if nothing had ever happened. What, I
asked myself, if there had been no Earth and no planets and no
stars and no space and no me to think about there being nothing and no me to think about there being no me to think about
there being nothing? Back and back I retreated in my mind,
dangerously, giddily seeking either an understanding of oblivion or some kind of solid wall at the back of a sensation of
nothingness that excluded even nothingness. There were times
when this peculiar, corkscrewing expedition would send my
brain spinning off into hazy perceptions of such a suffocating,
vacuum-like non-world that I had to hurry back to ordinariness
because I had become quite scared.

A similar but hopefully less neurotic process is required as
we set out on our journey through Mark's gospel. I don't think
we shall be frightened if we do this. I hope not, although a tinge
of fear is not always such a bad thing, but we may be a little
surprised by what we discover. I know, of course, that it will be
difficult – no, let us be honest, it will be impossible – to clear
our minds of all we think we know about the things that Jesus
said and did, but at least we can try.

You might, perfectly reasonably, ask the purpose of this
exercise. Well, all I can say is that every time I set out to read
one of the gospels, I seem to discover something that was not

there before but now is, or was there before and has now disappeared. Yes, I know that this is nonsense. The words don't change. But, quite apart from heavenly nudges and highlights, our minds naturally accept and reject and absorb and ignore as we read, and when all the bits and pieces that we retain are mixed with vague memories of what another person has said or written twenty-five years ago, or ten years ago or last week, the result is less than reliable.

This sort of thing happens with readers of my own books. For instance, after I have read a piece out loud in public, someone might very appreciatively ask which of my books it is taken from because they would like to take it home and read it for themselves. When I tell them the title of the book in which the passage appears they often look flabbergasted and assure me that they already own that book and have read it two or three times without ever noticing the bit that I've just been quoting.

The whole Bible is like that. We think we know, but we can be so wrong. That is very far from being a problem, though, wouldn't you agree? In fact, it can be most exciting and stimulating to keep coming back to familiar passages with our minds genuinely open to new ideas and insights. That is what we are going to do now with the gospel of Mark. What ideas and stories and memories will it spark for me – for you? What will it tell us about the message and the person of the great Servant King, Jesus Christ, the Son of God?

The Proclamation
of John the Baptist

1 : 2 – 8

As it is written in the prophet Isaiah, 'See, I am sending my messenger ahead of you, who will prepare your way; the voice of one crying out in the wilderness: "Prepare the way of the Lord, make his paths straight." '

John the baptizer appeared in the wilderness, proclaiming a baptism of repentance for the forgiveness of sins. And people from the whole Judean countryside and all the people of Jerusalem were going out to him, and were baptized by him in the river Jordan, confessing their sins. Now John was clothed with camel's hair, with a leather belt around his waist, and he ate locusts and wild honey.

He proclaimed, 'The one who is more powerful than I is coming after me; I am not worthy to stoop down and untie the thong of his sandals. I have baptized you with water; but he will baptize you with the Holy Spirit.'

No MESSING ABOUT WITH MARK, IS THERE? STRAIGHT ONTO centre-stage strides the striking figure of John the Baptizer, or John the Baptist, as most of us have always known him. One of my favourite characters in the New Testament, John is frequently portrayed as a hairy, wild-eyed head-case, snarling around the desert stuffing his face with insects and honey and putting on a sort of loony sideshow for the locals.

In fact, John was deadly serious about the job that he had been born for, absolutely determined to play out his role as the man chosen by God to prepare the way for the Messiah. Reading through all the gospel references to this extraordinary man recently (well worth the trouble, incidentally) I was struck by many things that I had not properly considered before. Let me share one or two of them with you.

First, he was such a practical and uncompromising moralist. After tearing the Pharisees and Sadducees off a strip (see the third chapter of Luke's gospel) he was asked specific questions about the sorts of changes in behaviour that should precede baptism. His fearsomely detailed replies suggest that John, like Jesus, might be less than popular in our modern western churches. Imagine if John the Baptist came to the local High Street church one Sunday morning and was asked similar questions by a bunch of people thinking of getting baptised. (All right, I know the theology and the order is wrong, but it might just as well be Jesus himself, and we're only pretending anyway.)

'What should we do?' they ask.

'Right!' says John briskly, 'if you've got two cars give one to a family that can't afford one, or, if you like, sell one of them and give the money to an aid agency or something. Some of you have got far too much money stashed away as well. God gave it to you to use for others. Are you going to?'

'What should I do?' asks another.

'Stop being selfish and ratty with your wife when no-one else is around and show a bit of affection,' suggests John.

'What about me?'

'Stop making excuses for not doing things in the church. Either help because you want to or tell them you're not going to.'

'And me?'

'Dump your pornography.'

'What about me?'

'Keep your promise about visiting the elderly lady next door every day. You've stopped going.'

Terrifying, isn't it? By the way, if you think I'm going to say where I come in that list, think again! Of course I made all that up. I have no idea what John or Jesus would say if they turned up in the flesh at my church or any other church. At the same time there's little doubt that we are low on practical morality, don't you think? In our modern, pussyfooting set-ups we Christians can get away with murder, or, at least, we can bury the body without being seen by anyone else – except Jesus.

Secondly, in stark contrast, and leaping ahead in the story, is that moment recorded in the eleventh chapter of Matthew's gospel when John, thrown into prison by Herod, and failing in confidence and self-belief, shows just how human and vulnerable he has become. He sends a sad little message to Jesus asking if he really is the Messiah. Or should they expect another?

The devil tells lies in the darkness, doesn't he?

How could John the Baptist *possibly* have ended up plummeting to such a depth of doubt and discouragement? After all, it wasn't long since he had been loudly proclaiming the need for repentance, aggressively taking on the Pharisees and Sadducees, and baptising hundreds in the Jordan. Not only that, but the Holy Spirit had enabled him to identify Jesus as the Messiah on the bank of that same river. He *knew* Jesus was the Messiah. Surely he did. Why on earth would he for one single moment believe that he should expect someone else?

The answer, of course, the sad and salutary truth, is that John was a mere man, and was therefore subject to all the fear and uneasiness that anyone would suffer when shut away from his place and his function and the light of the outside world.

The reply that Jesus sends to John about the lame walking and the deaf hearing and the dead being raised and the good news being preached is sometimes quoted by cynics as an example of the contradictions that are to be found in the Bible. Why, they want to know, does Jesus give a different answer to John than he gave to the Pharisees when they asked him the same question? He told them they wouldn't get a sign. Well, yes, the cynics are right. It is indeed just one example of the glorious, life-giving contradictions that offer evidence of the dynamic, inventive God that we try to serve. Jesus didn't want to comfort the Pharisees, but he did want to comfort John. Very soon he was to have similar experiences himself.

From certainty in morality and ministry to desolation and doubt in dark times. This is the way of the true believer and always has been. Take heart from this great man who prepared the way for his master, and if you are in darkness today, send a message out, then listen for a bespoke word of comfort from Jesus.

3

The Baptism of Jesus

1 : 9 – 11

In those days Jesus came from Nazareth of Galilee and was baptized by John in the Jordan. And just as he was coming up out of the water, he saw the heavens torn apart and the Spirit descending like a dove on him. And a voice came from heaven, 'You are my Son, the Beloved; with you I am well pleased.'

OVER THE YEARS MY WIFE AND I HAVE BEEN PRESENT AT baptisms, christenings, dedications, infant dramas, junior dramas, secondary school plays, one bar mitzvah, confirmations, football award evenings, eighteenth birthday parties, ordinations, graduation ceremonies, first nights, last nights and a multitude of dancing school presentations. One thing that all these events had in common was the presence of one or more proud parents gazing fondly at their offspring as they received awards or performed their piece or made a speech or got dunked in the font.

Here is a rather more significant example of such occasions. The proud father – it happens to be God in this case – rips apart the back-drop that constitutes the natural order of things so that he can express the passionate pleasure he takes in a son who has turned out exactly as he had hoped he would (every parent's dream, too often followed by a nightmare).

Doubtless, the other function of this very special family occasion was to encourage and reassure Jesus as he prepared to embark on a period of ministry that was destined to affect the eternal lives of billions of men and women. And, my goodness, he must have needed it, don't you think? You will be as familiar as I am with the sensation of doom-laden wretchedness that envelops us as we get closer and closer to some awful event or encounter that simply cannot be avoided however much we dread it. Giving a speech, going into hospital, visiting the dentist, there is a lengthy list and it varies for each one of us. Each of the dark, drudging days leading up to such horrors can be an echoing cavern of misery. What point is there in being alive when next Thursday refuses to go away?

For Jesus the future must have been terrifying. Three years of exhaustingly hard work, continual conflict, constant resistance to temptation and the profound loneliness of never really being fully understood, were to end in torture and death at the hands of the very people he had come to rescue. Yes, of course it would be worth it. Of course it would. But what a prospect! If ever a willing son needed a warm word of confidence and affirmation it was now.

Why was God so pleased with his son? Well, apart from anything else, he had certainly loved him through eternity.

'Before Abraham was,' Jesus tells an infuriated bunch of listeners in the eighth chapter of John's gospel, 'I am.'

Let us not pretend to even partially understand this. I am constantly amazed by the way in which some people talk about such mystical matters as though the comprehension of them is the least of their problems. All we can confidently say is that, in some mysterious way, Jesus had always been alive, he was with God, he was part of God, he was God, he was loved by God. So, in that sense, God would certainly have been pleased with him.

I suspect, though, that the primary issue here was obedience.

As we travel through the gospel of Mark, or any other gospel for that matter, we are going to be faced again and again with the incontrovertible fact that Jesus was truly man, and was therefore tempted as a man. We are not talking about some first-century Clark Kent. We are talking about the impossible but essential paradox of a person who really, really was God, as well as really, really being a man. If he was a real man the implication is clear, isn't it? Jesus could have disobeyed God. He could have screwed the whole thing up. So far, he hadn't, and his father was very proud and very pleased.

While we're on the subject of obedience, do you remember that famous passage in John's gospel where Jesus has just spoken to the Samaritan woman by the well, and the disciples, returning from a food-buying expedition, encourage him to eat?

'I have food you know nothing about,' says Jesus. 'My food is to do the will of the one who sent me.'

His food was obedience. Perhaps we need a change of diet. It appears that doing what we are told will build us up and make us strong. I would love my heavenly Father to be well pleased with me, wouldn't you?

4

The Temptation of Jesus

1 : 12 – 13
And the Spirit immediately drove him out into the wilderness. He was in the wilderness forty days, tempted by Satan; and he was with the wild beasts; and the angels waited on him.

HERE WE FOCUS EVEN MORE NARROWLY ON THESE ISSUES OF obedience and the humanity of Jesus.

I remember reading somewhere about a group of nuns who

were being asked about the human aspects of Jesus. They agreed that he must have experienced temptation in all the same areas as other human beings – except one. These ladies simply could not bring themselves to believe that their master ever experienced sexual temptation. I can understand why they felt like that. Sex and the Son of God do not sit very happily together in our imaginations. The fact is, though, that the divinity of Jesus was never so apparent as when he triumphed in his humanity. He was, in a sense, God's second shot at creating a man who might retain and reflect the image of God in which he had been made without allowing that image to be tarnished by sin. Adam was the first, and, as we all know, he failed.

In the wilderness, Jesus, carrying his divinity like a backpack, had to face and resist the gritty temptations that we all face, sexual temptation included. And his mission was to achieve this, not by opening his backpack and throwing a few divine explosives around like that lunatic wizard in Monty Python and the Holy Grail, but as an act of obedience performed by a human being in deference to his God. We shall never fully comprehend this because, quite apart from the cloud of paradoxes that engulf us when we try, we have no idea what it means to have such power available and choose not to employ it. On the other hand, it might increase our appreciation of the sacrifice Jesus made for us, to understand that this platform for his ministry, this victory over temptation, was the product of very basic, very human sweat and determination.

Perish the thought, but imagine for a moment that Jesus had been able to appear on the Parkinson show, happily sandwiched between Dolly Parton and Ben Elton.

'What gave you most satisfaction in those famous three years of yours?' Parkinson might ask. 'The miracles, perhaps?'

What would Jesus say? I think he might make the point that, in one sense, the miracles were the easy part. Exhausting yes, but where faith met willingness there was nothing to prevent his Father from performing a miracle. Those forty days in the desert, though; that moment when Peter tried to persuade him that he needn't go through with the crucifixion; that night in Gethsemane – those were the make-or-break times, the gritted-teeth times, the times when it might have been easier to give in than to do the right thing. Satisfaction certainly, but only in knowing that he had gone on making the right choices right up to the end.

I feel absolutely sure that Dolly and Ben would have been entranced.

5

The Beginning of
the Galilean Ministry

1 : 14 – 15

Now after John was arrested, Jesus came to Galilee, proclaiming the good news of God, and saying, 'The time is fulfilled, and the kingdom of God has come near; repent, and believe in the good news.'

WITH A GREAT DEAL MORE SKILL AND ALACRITY THAN THE British sprint relay team in the 2001 Athletic World Championships, Jesus took the baton of good news from John. But here is the question we should have asked right at the beginning:

What *is* this good news?

What is the good news of the gospel that Jesus urged and urges us all to believe in?

'Oh, no!' I hear some of you groan. 'Here he goes again – asking a question with a perfectly obvious answer, and probably taking several hundred words to do it.'

Well, I'm sorry, but I'm not sure this question does have an obvious answer, or perhaps I should say, an answer that genuinely means something to ordinary old human beings like me, and a significant percentage of you.

With the help of my trusty concordance (you need no previous knowledge of music to use one, by the way), I have looked up other references to Good News in the Bible. One of them is a passage from Acts where Luke offers this information:

> Now those who had been scattered by the persecution of Stephen travelled as far as Phoenicia, Cyprus and Antioch, telling the message only to Jews. Some of them, however, men from Cyprus and Cyrene, went to Antioch and began to speak to Greeks also, telling them the good news about the Lord Jesus.

Does the question not explode into your face like a game-bird rocketing out of cover? *What* good news? What was it? What was the good news that these associates of Stephen were so keen to share with the Greeks? By this time Jesus was long dead. They had just seen Stephen, their fellow-Christian, reduced to a bloodied, lifeless heap because of his adherence to The Way. Clearly, that was why these men had scattered – to avoid the same fate. Who can blame them? Surely they would now have the good sense to lie low in some quiet cave in the middle of nowhere, forgetting everything they had ever known about Jesus, and claiming to be third generation camel-worshippers if visitors happened to question their religious affiliation.

What was the good news?

It can't have *just* been that Stephen's face was shining even as he died, can it? Impressive as that fact undoubtedly is, it must have been less than effective as an evangelistic ploy.

'Hey, listen, chaps! Good news! If you become a Christian you may well be pounded to death with rocks, but you'll be smiling as it happens ...'

No, that can't be the good news.

A friend rang while I was thinking about this, so I asked him what kind of good news *he* thought these men might have been spreading.

'The good news that they'd escaped?' he suggested.

Why do I bother asking my flippant friends anything?

So, come on! When the founder of your faith has been killed on a cross and his posthumous followers are harassed, persecuted and murdered, what is the good news? When the spiritual concepts that you want to communicate are offensive to Jews and inexplicable to Greeks, what is the good news? When, in present-day situations, our faith by no means guarantees us rescue from bereavement, hardship and disaster, what is the good news? When Christianity presents us with a life-long storm of a struggle to even dimly comprehend who we are, who God is, and what the nature of the relationship between the two should be, what is the good news? When churches and denominations fight and argue and present a raggedly negative face to the rest of the world, what is the good news? When each of us looks into his or her own heart and, all too often, sees sin where there should be virtue and doubt where there should be faith, what is the good news?

Yes, go on, please interrupt me. Take out your neatly packed theological parcels, the ones labelled Redemption and Justification and Salvation and Eternal Life. You will not hear me argue with you about the central importance of those concepts to the Christian faith. They have changed the world for millions and will continue to do so. But look, I am a human being, and because of that the good news that I can't help sharing cannot be less ordinary or more exciting or less closely linked to life here on earth than anything else I have ever experienced. It thrills my soul, but it still lacks shape.

What then? What is in my heart?

I have met this man called Jesus who, as this passage tells us, stepped out to deliver the good news two thousand years ago. My spirit tells me that he has all the answers I shall ever need, even if he will not give them to me now. Like Peter splashing to the shore from his fishing boat I shall run to him one day when I spy him in the distance because I want so much to be with him. I shall have breakfast with him – he will cook it. He has made it possible for me to go to a place where the past cannot strangle the present, and bodies cannot wear out, and tears will be wiped away, and sins will be forgiven, and relationships will be healed, and we shall be very much ourselves, and things will be as they were always intended to be, and we shall be in the place that we were homesick for but could not identify and there will be no more religion and it will be divinely ordinary.

We shall be happy and at home. Good news for God, and good news for us. In my best and most sane moments – that is what is in my heart.

6

Jesus Calls the First Disciples

1 : 16 – 20

As Jesus passed along the Sea of Galilee, he saw Simon and his brother Andrew casting a net into the sea — for they were fishermen. And Jesus said to them, 'Follow me and I will make you fish for people.' And immediately they left their nets and followed him. As he went a little farther, he saw James son of Zebedee and his brother John, who were in their boat mending the nets. Immediately he called them; and they left their father Zebedee in the boat with the hired men, and followed him.

NOWADAYS PEOPLE SEEM TO CHANGE CAREERS QUITE OFTEN, don't they? But I am quite sure that Simon and Andrew and James and John never dreamed that the future could hold anything but fishing – for fish, that is. Then, amazingly, they were called out of being what they were and taken in a completely different direction. A lot of the people that I meet, Christians and non-Christians, find it very difficult to believe that they really can be called by Jesus out of the limitations and the habits and the shapes of behaviour that have grown and combined over the years to make them what they are.

Looking back into my own life for examples of this, I found myself recalling childhood events that were like templates cut into my life, patterns that threatened to be repeated endlessly as the years went by. One memory that rather surprised me when it surfaced was established during a trip to Austria when I was twelve, a trip whose origins lay, rather bizarrely, in one fleeting moment when I was deeply worried that I might be a direct descendant of Adolf Hitler.

I think I had better explain that.

I was born a few years after the war had ended. Naturally, in the course of my growing-up, there was much relieved and animated talk among family and friends about the mad dictator and the way in which his power-crazed attempts to take over the world had been foiled by the allies. This was exciting and unthreatening, the war being well and truly over, but in a separate, unrelated conversation I overheard my father casually mention that his grandfather had been an Austrian house-painter. With a small boy's disregard for clear and contradictory issues of time and space, I felt my blood run cold. The German dictator had been an Austrian house-painter. Could I be Adolf Hitler's great-grandson!

Learning through frantically urgent enquiries that I was mistaken in this appalling assumption was like a cold shower on a blazing hot day, despite the laughter that seemed to continue for ever. Such relief! But a heavy residue of interest remained. My ancestral roots were in the soil of a far-off country. At the age of twelve I begged my parents to let me go on a school trip to Austria.

I went.

Guidelines sent out to parents by the school suggested that each boy would need no more than five pounds pocket money for the whole trip. My mother and father were not well off, and five pounds was quite a lot of money in those days, so that was exactly the amount I took. Five pounds! It seemed a fortune to me. I had never owned so much in my life. I was amazed to discover that some other boys had brought ten, fifteen or even twenty pounds.

I managed my money very badly. By the second day I had spent every penny of my five pounds on sweets and drinks and a gift for my mother. I didn't tell anyone that my supply of pocket-money had run out. Salzburg and Innsbruck and all the mountains and the lakes were lovely to look at, but I grew very weary of pretending that I didn't want anything when the others went into shops. I felt like a non-reader forced to spend time with scholars in a library. It was a subtle but profound experience of not belonging.

A couple of days before the end of our holiday the teacher in charge called the group together for a 'special' talk. He announced that he had a decision to make, and that we must all be involved in that decision. We formed an intrigued circle in the sitting-room of the youth hostel.

'It's about Paul,' he said, tilting his head towards the boy sitting rather self-consciously beside him. 'Paul tells me he's run out of pocket-money. Well, there are still two days to go, so here's my suggestion. I've got some extra money left from what your parents paid. Should we give Paul a little bit of that to keep him going for the rest of the holiday? It's your money really, so it's up to you.'

Boys of that age can be gooily sentimental at times. Solemn headshakes, murmurs of approval and smiles of reassurance for good old Paul were very much the order of the day. This happened a long time ago, but I know for sure that, like Timothy Winters in Charles Causley's poem, no-one would have nodded more solemnly, murmured more approvingly or smiled more reassuringly than the twelve-year-old Adrian Plass. Of course poor, stony-broke Paul must have a hand-out from the common fund. It was only right. I truly believed that.

The other thing I know for sure is that it never occurred to me for one second that I was in the same sinking financial boat as Paul, nor that I was just as entitled to a helping hand as he was. He had probably run out of money the day before. I had been penniless for days. Strangely, it was not until years later that I was suddenly struck by these undeniable facts. It was as though I regarded the feelings and experiences and ideas of my inner life as a sort of fiction, whereas the concerns of others were non-fiction, touching on, engaging with and being affected by the real world.

The general principles of that early experience were repeated in various forms again and again until I reached my late thirties. One day, that cave-bound inner life was coaxed and called out into the open air by, I believe, the same person who called these four fishermen. Having emerged, it took a deep breath and decided to stay. I became a writer, and, in a way, I have been allowed to do my own bit of fishing, for which I sincerely thank God.

If he does call you, do find out what he wants from you. It will change your life.

The Man with an Unclean Spirit

1 : 21 – 28

They went to Capernaum; and when the Sabbath came, he entered the synagogue and taught. They were astounded at his teaching, for he taught them as one having authority, and not as the scribes.

Just then there was in their synagogue a man with an unclean spirit, and he cried out, 'What have you to do with us, Jesus of Nazareth? Have you come to destroy us? I know who you are, the Holy One of God.'

But Jesus rebuked him, saying, 'Be silent, and come out of him!'

And the unclean spirit, convulsing him and crying with a loud voice, came out of him. They were all amazed, and they kept on asking one another, 'What is this? A new teaching — with authority! He commands even the unclean spirits, and they obey him.'

At once his fame began to spread throughout the surrounding region of Galilee.

I HAVE NEVER FOUND IT DIFFICULT TO UNDERSTAND WHY perfectly sane men and women get caught up in sects and cults led by powerful charismatic figures. Mankind is constantly searching for someone who speaks with real authority. I suppose that is part of the reason why invented figures such as Sherlock Holmes have always been so popular. An individual who genuinely and consistently appears to know what we should say and do and think offers a welcome refuge from a world characterised by mistrust, uncertainty and raggedness.

Is it possible that a lot of our fictional creations are manifestations of a universal, unconscious attempt to reconstruct or find substitutes for this Jesus, the man who was God become man, the only person in the history of the world whose FBI dirt-file would be completely empty, and who could be entrusted with your very soul because his story was not a story but a mind-blowing fact.

Robin Hood, Sir Galahad, Ivanhoe, Buck Rogers, Zorro, Dan Dare, Biggles, Roy of the Rovers, the Lone Ranger, the entire Mission Impossible team, Batman, Superman, Spiderman, Captain Kirk and Doctor Who. The list is rather dated, not just because I am dated as well, but because the age of the anti-hero is upon us, although the popularity of Harry Potter suggests that the public still craves its virtuous heroes. All of the people on that list of mine, and all the ones I'm sure I've forgotten that you can fill in for yourselves, combine qualities of goodness, incorruptibility and infinite resourcefulness. More than one of them regularly saved the world. Buck Rogers did it every Saturday morning. We paid a shilling to watch it. Biggles and Algy and Bertie and Ginger did it in every other book. Dan Dare was always doing it. Superman made a second profession out of it. Captain Kirk and Doctor Who between them must have saved the planet on countless occasions, many more times than Jesus. He only saved it once, but it wasn't on television or in a book or at the cinema. It was for real.

As we continue through this gospel we shall have an increasing sense, like the people who were privileged to witness this amazing healing, of the powerful authority that emanated and still emanates from the personality of Jesus, an authority that is able to promise us a 'happy ever after' ending that goes way beyond anything mere fiction can offer.

Jesus Heals Many at Simon's House

1 : 29 – 34

As soon as they left the synagogue, they entered the house of Simon and Andrew, with James and John. Now Simon's mother-in-law was in bed with a fever, and they told him about her at once. He came and took her by the hand and lifted her up. Then the fever left her, and she began to serve them.

That evening, at sundown, they brought to him all who were sick or possessed with demons. And the whole city was gathered around the door. And he cured many who were sick with various diseases, and cast out many demons; and he would not permit the demons to speak, because they knew him.

HOW FRUSTRATING FOR SIMON'S MOTHER-IN-LAW TO KNOW that Jesus was in her house and that her fever was making it impossible to get up and look after him. He knew how she was feeling, of course, and do you detect, as I do, a hint of respect and closeness in that little nugget of information about him taking her hand and lifting her up? I know that the phrase is used elsewhere in the gospels, but there is an elegance and, perhaps, an exchanged smile in the middle of all that somewhere.

The lesson that is frequently drawn from this account of the healing of Simon's mother-in-law is about God healing us so that we will then be able to serve him. A perfectly good point to make, of course, but I suspect that there is an even more important lesson to be learned. You see, I have no doubt at all that Simon's mother-in-law was in the habit of serving on a day-to-day basis. It was part of what she was. Being healed simply released her to be herself.

Let us take courage, all those of us who feel that we have been pushed into a strange and alien shape by the expectations of those who see conformity as a priority. Conformity is very far from being the priority of the Holy Spirit. When God heals our bodies or our minds or our spirits, his aim is not to suppress our special characteristics, but to set us free to be ourselves in the best and most useful way possible.

Now that is what I *call* good news.

9

A Preaching Tour in Galilee

1 : 35 – 39

In the morning, while it was still very dark, he got up and went out to a deserted place, and there he prayed. And Simon and his companions hunted for him.

When they found him, they said to him, 'Everyone is searching for you.'

He answered, 'Let us go on to the neighboring towns, so that I may proclaim the message there also; for that is what I came out to do.'

And he went throughout Galilee, proclaiming the message in their synagogues and casting out demons.

ONE THING STRIKES ME IMMEDIATELY ABOUT THIS PASSAGE. Jesus doesn't seem to have changed much since he was a boy, does he? His disappearance in the dark, chilly morning and the way in which Simon and the others had to hunt for him, carry echoes of that other time, many years earlier, when the twelve-year-old Jesus did the same thing to his parents. He just slipped away and disappeared. That's what he did then, and that's what he was doing now. In fact, as I spend a moment thinking through the gospel accounts, I become aware that he did quite a lot of disappearing, usually to think and pray, as far as one can tell, occasionally to rest or grieve. It was a pattern in his life, and, presumably, an essential one.

So what was happening on this particular morning? They say it is idle to speculate but it's fun to be idle sometimes. Let us speculate.

Jesus wakes in the early hours of the morning after a very short sleep. Perhaps he lies awake for some time, thinking through the events of the previous day. The whole of the important city of Capernaum had been at his door. The *whole* city! Many healings and a lot of deliverance. So many people. Hoards of other desperate folk were bound to turn up throughout the next day as news of the miracles spread. In the face of such overwhelming need, surely it would make sense to simply continue his ministry in the same place on the following day.

And yet ...

There is a whisper in his ear, a voice reminding him that the obvious thing is not always the right thing, and the wrong thing is helpful neither to God nor to man. So, should he stay or should he go?

The answer to that question was to be found in only one place. Silently, moving with great care so as to wake nobody else, he rises and, wrapping his cloak around his shoulders, slips out into the open air. In a solitary place, somewhere where there will be no distractions, he seeks his Father's will and assurance. By the time the bewildered disciples locate him, long after the sun has crept over the rocky horizon, the decision is made.

Time for a tour of the provinces, and – puzzling for the disciples, no doubt – at a time when the West End run was going so well. The crowds were calling for more and more, and perhaps Jesus was tempted to give them what they wanted. Ultimately, though, he never allowed himself to be motivated by applause, nor popularity, nor even blatant need. He only did what he saw his Father doing. He knew why he was here, and that pre-dawn rendezvous had clarified and confirmed his spiritual instincts. It was time to go.

Earlier on I was saying that some childhood experiences are like templates cut into our lives, causing negative patterns to be repeated, and I offered the example of something that happened to me in Austria when I was twelve.

This pattern of disappearance in Jesus' life has got me thinking about the template business all over again. I'm not surprised. Reading about Jesus often stirs things up.

I grew up in a house at the bottom of one of the posher streets in our village. Many of the people who lived in Longmeads (the name of our road) were very self-consciously aware that they did *not* live in a scrubby council estate at the other end of the village. Every house in our road was privately owned, and every garden was manicured in that nervously defensive, fussily middle-class way that is particularly English.

In the house next to ours lived Mr and Mrs Jones. He was a teacher and she was a housewife. She was nice and friendly. He was not. In what way not? Well, I had two brothers, one older and one younger. We played constantly in the garden. We played football and cricket and French cricket and a sort of shrunken version of tennis, and we sometimes played an exciting game which involved throwing a tennis ball right over the house so that the person on the other side waited for it to fall out of the sky and tried to catch it. We played in the back garden and we played in the front. Naturally, balls of various shapes and sizes were required for these activities.

From the very beginning Mr Jones *never* let us have our ball back when it crossed the fence into his garden.

We certainly didn't intend our precious footballs or tennis balls to trespass in his sacred domain. Indeed, every time we began another game we assured each other that under no circumstances would such an inconvenient thing be allowed to happen. It did, of course. Small boys may promise themselves and each other the world, but once the game gets going such considerations tend to evaporate. It made Mr Jones very cross. He *would not* give anything back. We could only retrieve our ball by sneaking over the fence when he wasn't looking. My flesh crawls as I recollect undertaking these desperate commando exercises when it was my turn because I was the one who had 'done it'.

In the house connected to ours on the other side lived Sheila Bourne, a lady who bore a striking resemblance to Queen Elizabeth. Mrs Bourne was a nurse, and seemed, on the rare occasions when we encountered her, to be very nice, if a little stern. The trouble was that she was a *night* nurse. She worked during the night and slept during the day. Aware as my mother must have been that there was nothing intrinsically wrong with little boys making noise in the course of their play, she constantly worried that our whooping and yelling would wake Sheila, who had apparently complained once or twice that she had been unable to sleep because of our raised voices.

'Sheila's asleep! Play quietly! You'll have to come in if you can't keep the noise down.'

During the long holidays my poor mother got quite neurotic about it, and, of course, passed a share of her tension to us. Imagine us three boys battling to keep our ball from flying over the hedge on one side, and, at the same time, doing our inadequate best to play a hissed, whispering game of football or cricket?

Talk about templates!

Moving into our present house has allowed these memories to surface. For the first time we are in a detached house with no neighbours at all on one side and nothing but fields and distant horizon at the back. We can play music as loudly as we want without worrying about how it affects others. To the small boy in me it feels like a crime – but it's not. Then, soon after we moved in, two anxious-looking little boys from the house next to us appeared on our front step to nervously enquire if they might get their ball back from our garden.

The old choice – revenge or healing?

'Yes,' I said, 'you can get your ball, and I don't care how many times it comes into our garden. You can always fetch it without having to ask. Even if it comes over a *million* times you can still come and get it back.'

Slightly puzzled, but beaming with pleasure, they went to collect their ball.

'Never let your play impinge on others, and keep your voice down in case someone's trying to sleep.'

There were many positive patterns formed in my early life, but I am surprised to find, on reflection, the extent to which this particular template has negatively affected my friendships, my marriage, my confidence and my faith. However, a process of healing has been going on for a long time, and God wastes nothing. Give God your dark side. He will rig a few lamps up and use it for something.

10

Jesus Cleanses a Leper

1 : 40 – 45

A leper came to him begging him, and kneeling he said to him, 'If you choose, you can make me clean.'

Moved with pity, Jesus stretched out his hand and touched him, and said to him, 'I do choose. Be made clean!'

Immediately the leprosy left him, and he was made clean. After sternly warning him he sent him away at once, saying to him,

'See that you say nothing to anyone; but go, show yourself to the priest, and offer for your cleansing what Moses commanded, as a testimony to them.'

But he went out and began to proclaim it freely, and to spread the word, so that Jesus could no longer go into a town openly, but stayed out in the country; and people came to him from every quarter.

W HAT A NIGHTMARE JESUS WOULD HAVE BEEN TO YOUR typical modern publicist. A very frustrating potential client indeed. All that hypothetical income thrown away because he simply would not build on his strengths.

Dear J.C. (*writes our first century Max Clifford*),

One of our people did lunch with one of your people on Friday. Can't recall the name – treasurer for your outfit I gather. Certainly seems to be the only one of your crew with his head screwed on properly if you don't mind me saying so. I don't know if he had your authorisation, but he was floating the idea of me setting up something for you on the publicity front.

Okay, I know a bit about your work, and I've given the matter some thought, so why don't we throw out a few nuts and see if the squirrels take 'em.

J.C. I'd like to take you on because, frankly, you've got some very good stuff. I mean, up-front compassion is definitely, absolutely in, and I have to say you do the deeply sincere thing better than anyone else on my books. And then there's the healings. Oh, man! The healings are the best part of the act. They are just *terrific*! Properly handled, a little goldmine. Not quite so many would be good. Always leave 'em wanting more, I say. Lose the 'your sins are forgiven' angle and a bit more Spielberg in the presentation would be helpful, but I could really milk those healings of yours, J.C. In fact, I'd go so far as to say that, with a little stimulation of the market, you and me could be enjoying double cream and strawberry jam on our scones every single night.

Then we've got those nice little stories you do – could be

spiced up a bit, but very nice – we've got the trick with the bread, the water into wine, the walking on the water illusion, the old coin in the mouth of the fish scam – I don't know how you do 'em, but it's all rattling good stuff. And, I tell you, J.C., I don't know who writes for you, but your spiel is top of the range, mate.

So, given all that, what I cannot get my head round is, *why* do you not make the most of it? Why not cash in? It's beyond me. What is the point of every single time telling the punters you've healed to keep their mouths shut? What is wrong with you, compadre? What we in the business call 'strategic humility' is one thing – I can always use that as well – but chucking your chances down the drain is another. If you're planning to do the humble thing you make sure it happens somewhere where you know you're going to be seen, don't you?

The thing I heard about this leper today is a case in point. When he got on to you about sorting him out the right line would have been, 'Yes, I am prepared to do the business, but nothing's free in this world, chum. Putting you right is conditional on you dropping a word in the ears of certain people listed on the contract that I will now ask you to stick your mark on.' Get my drift? Use the old noddle – the old grey matter.

Couple more things, old son. Don't waste your time with the small venues and the small people, stop getting up the noses of important movers and shakers who could do you a bit of good if they were to feel so inclined, add a bit of class to those rough, fishy old roadies of yours, dump the religious angle because – trust me – it never got anyone anywhere, and I can see you (and me – fair dos!) cleaning up in a big way. I honestly can. Just give me a bell if you ever decide to look at what you're doing and really start taking it seriously …

Yours etc.

'Not by might, nor by power, nor by the services of a publicity agent, but by my Spirit,' says the Lord.

Some things, thank God, will never change.

Jesus Heals the Paralytic

2 : 1 – 12

When he returned to Capernaum after some days, it was reported that he was at home. So many gathered around that there was no longer room for them, not even in front of the door; and he was speaking the word to them. Then some people came, bringing to him a paralysed man, carried by four of them. And when they could not bring him to Jesus because of the crowd, they removed the roof above him; and after having dug through it, they let down the mat on which the paralytic lay.

When Jesus saw their faith, he said to the paralytic, 'Son, your sins are forgiven.'

Now some of the scribes were sitting there, questioning in their hearts, 'Why does this fellow speak in this way? It is blasphemy! Who can forgive sins but God alone?'

At once Jesus perceived in his spirit that they were discussing these questions among themselves; and he said to them, 'Why do you raise such questions in your hearts? Which is easier, to say to the paralytic, "Your sins are forgiven," or to say, "Stand up and take your mat and walk"? But so that you may know that the Son of Man has authority on earth to forgive sins' – he said to the paralytic – 'I say to you, stand up, take your mat and go to your home.'

And he stood up, and immediately took the mat and went out before all of them; so that they were all amazed and glorified God, saying, 'We have never seen anything like this!'

THERE IS A HEART OF AUTHENTICITY IN PROFOUND NEED that always seemed to appeal to Jesus. Again and again we read of occasions when he responded positively to the passion or ingenuity with which sick and needy folk pressed themselves upon him. Such a list, quite apart from the incident recorded here, would include Jairus seeking help on behalf of his daughter, the woman who touched the hem of Jesus' garment, blind Bartimaeus, the father of the boy whom the disciples were unable to heal and the Syrophoenician woman who so wittily and successfully importuned Jesus in the matter of her daughter's unclean spirit.

The single-tracked, intense determination of these people was consistently rewarded. It was as though extreme suffering, either in oneself or on behalf of another, had a purifying effect on the motivational spirit with which these petitioners approached the master. Perhaps the idea I am stumbling slowly towards is the notion that, living in such an authentic manner himself, Jesus respected the reality and depth of their need. Worth remembering perhaps in our modern discussions about healing.

He also reacted very well to sheer cheek. These four fellows digging a hole in the roof and (literally) jumping the long, rumbustious queue by letting their mate down on a stretcher strikes me as a very 'laddish' thing to do. It could have turned out to be a very bad idea, couldn't it? We go along with the way in which Jesus reacted because – well, because he was Jesus. But there is a far from insignificant element in the church today who, given the beginning of this little story and asked to guess the end, might well have supposed that Jesus would have looked up through the hole in the roof and addressed these cheeky chaps in the following manner:

'Right, you four men, you can take those silly grins off your faces for a start. Healing is no laughing matter. Okay, couple of points. Although I do, of course, understand and appreciate your concern for your friend, there is a *right* way of doing things and there is a *wrong* way. This, I am very much afraid, is the wrong way. First of all, have you considered the fact that you have caused criminal damage to the roof of a house that does not belong to you? No, I didn't think you had. Stewardship? Concern for others? Eh? There is absolutely no question of you being allowed access to me through such an unkind and thoughtless act.

'Secondly, you cannot fail to be aware that this place is full of people waiting to be healed, and a very long line has been forming outside since dawn. Can you honestly justify your blatant attempt to cheat those who have been waiting so patiently by sneaking your friend in through the roof so that he is at the front of the queue instead of the back? Can you? Well, can you? No, I thought not.

'Right – things to do. You pull him back *up*. You find the owner of the house, you apologise and pay him for the damage to his roof, and then you join the queue outside at the very back, collect a number from Peter, and, as you wait your turn you *think about what you've done*. Off you go. Next!'

Which Jesus would you rather have? No contest really, is there?

It strikes me, by the way, that one of the things the scribes probably hated most about Jesus was that he *liked* people. Ugh!

12

Jesus Calls Levi

2 : 13 – 17

Jesus went out again beside the sea; the whole crowd gathered around him, and he taught them. As he was walking along, he saw Levi son of Alphaeus sitting at the tax booth, and he said to him, 'Follow me.' And he got up and followed him.

And as he sat at dinner in Levi's house, many tax collectors and sinners were also sitting with Jesus and his disciples — for there were many who followed him.

When the scribes of the Pharisees saw that he was eating with sinners and tax collectors, they said to his disciples, 'Why does he eat with tax collectors and sinners?'

When Jesus heard this, he said to them, 'Those who are well have no need of a physician, but those who are sick; I have come to call not the righteous but sinners.'

Pretty good ploy this on Jesus' part, don't you think? I don't know if Zaccheus or Levi came first, but the pattern seems to be the same. Save a tax collector and you get asked to dinner. Only joking. I'm sure it never crossed his mind. Well – almost sure.

Jesus' desire and willingness to move right into the homes and hearts of the sad, the bad and the greedy was and is a jewel in the crown of his ministry. The Pharisees were quite unable to accept it, and I imagine one or two of the sinners had a bit of a problem taking it in. They still do. I still do sometimes.

I remember, for instance, a particular fortnight around the end of August and beginning of September in the first year of this century.

The year had begun with the sad death of our dear dog, Rosie, who had grown up with our children, but, being in the midst of hectic preparations for the blessing of my oldest son's marriage, we barely had a moment to mourn her passing. Matthew had married his charming Azeri bride, Alina, briefly and technically in Turkey earlier that year. Now they were anxious to do the thing properly, and they wanted 'the works'. They wanted to be married by a proper vicar in a proper country church, wearing proper wedding clothes with proper guests and a proper wedding reception afterwards. And, of course, ideally it would happen on a proper sunny English day in early September.

Their wishes were granted. That year the second of September was one of those perfect days when nothing goes wrong and the laughter and tears and other weather all happen in just the right places. It couldn't have been more – proper.

A thrilling facet of this sparkling jewel of an occasion was the presence of Alina's parents, Irina and Oleg, who flew all the way from Baku, the capital of Azerbaijan, on the evening before the wedding, to be with their daughter on her special day. Azerbaijan is a beaurocratic nightmare. Arranging visas and tickets had been a long, exhausting business for us all. But now, excitingly, if improbably, these two non-English-speaking inhabitants of an oil-producing ex-Soviet republic were comfortably ensconced in a farmhouse bed and breakfast establishment just down the road. Unbelievable!

It was in the week after the wedding that my neurosis began to set in. Our house had been occupied and eaten in every day by at least ten people, sometimes twelve. This was fine except that I am famous – or rather infamous – for my dislike of clutter and untidiness. Members of my family alternate between derision and annoyance in their response to this aspect of my personality, but there's nothing I can do about it, I'm afraid. I am capable of a sort of cataclysmic untidiness of my own on rare occasions, but the point is that I select those occasions, if you see what I mean.

During that second week I began to understand how servants working in large houses in the Victorian and Edwardian eras must have felt during every day of their lives. Hoovering and washing-up and laying tables and putting things away and preparing meals and taking rubbish to the council tip and shopping and sorting everything out was exhausting. Not, I hasten to add, in case my wife reads this, that I laboured alone. We all worked hard. No, it was just that this completion neurosis of mine drove me past the point of reasonable endeavour, producing a state of wild-eyed frustration in me whenever some innocent soul committed the unforgivable sin of moving a coffee table five degrees away from an exact right-angle, or placed a coffee-cup on a polished surface without using a coaster. Sad, isn't it?

For the first few days of this feverish activity, though I say it myself, I handled things pretty well. I quite enjoyed an inner, heroic posturing in the role of one working selflessly for the sake of others. I was the host who not only welcomed and entertained, but also laboured ceaselessly behind the scenes with no thought of reward or gratitude. How impressed they must be, I reflected, by the way the house is magically sorted out in their absence each day, calm and ordered in readiness for their return. A good witness too, I thought smugly (may God forgive me!), for Christians to offer those from a distant, pagan land.

At around lunchtime on the thirteenth day I simply ran out of steam and goodwill. Why the dickens was I bothering to clean up after people who just came in and messed it all up again? What was the point? When were they going to acknowledge the hard work I'd been doing? They probably hadn't even noticed. Huh! Fancy coming all this way from a foreign country and letting me slave away like a – like a slave. I felt tired and irritable and fed-up ...

That morning I sat at my desk, head in hands, surveying the wreckage of my good intentions and the disintegration of my so-called Christian witness. The dwelling place of my faith was in a state of complete disarray, quite unsuitable for visitors. It was at that moment that the gentle voice of Jesus said, very quietly, 'May I come in?'

'Well,' I replied, almost tearfully, 'it's a bit of a mess, actually.'

'Oh, I've never minded that,' he said, 'I'll give you a hand clearing up.'

'Thank you,' I said, and I meant it.

He calls on the strangest people at the strangest times, doesn't he?

Ready?

The Question about Fasting

2 : 18 – 22

Now John's disciples and the Pharisees were fasting; and people came and said to him, 'Why do John's disciples and the disciples of the Pharisees fast, but your disciples do not fast?'

Jesus said to them, 'The wedding guests cannot fast while the bridegroom is with them, can they? As long as they have the bridegroom with them, they cannot fast. The days will come when the bridegroom is taken away from them, and then they will fast on that day.

'No one sews a piece of unshrunk cloth on an old cloak; otherwise, the patch pulls away from it, the new from the old, and a worse tear is made. And no one puts new wine into old wineskins; otherwise, the wine will burst the skins, and the wine is lost, and so are the skins; but one puts new wine into fresh wineskins.'

FOR THE DISCIPLES OF JESUS TO FAST WOULD HAVE BEEN LIKE travelling an entire circuit of the world in order to visit the person in the house next door. A waste of time and energy. As the master says here, there would be plenty of time and necessity for that after his death. The bridegroom knew full well that before very long his bride would be widowed for a season.

This passage highlights an interesting and continual tension between celebration and denial in the life of Jesus. His enjoyment of parties, people and the occasional spot of luxury overlaps and intertwines with the hard work and restraint that his ministry demanded, and both were essential elements in the person that he happily made visible to the world. The former was never allowed to eclipse or detract from the latter, but I find it fascinating to observe how these two aspects of his approach to life were so very comfortably twinned.

Incidentally, the fasting or not fasting issue reminds me (and I am certainly not the first person to make this observation) that there is an awful lot of eating in the New Testament, and that Jesus is usually right at the centre of it.

I was once interviewed in Europe by a journalist who worked for a liberal Christian newspaper. Liberals can be as narrow and severe about the breadth of their views as any grim, tight-lipped nonconformist, and this reporter was no exception. He and I were sitting in a café with a friend of mine. Before us on a table stood a tray bearing pots of tea and a plate containing some little cakes.

'Do you believe,' he asked, 'that here in this café is church? You and me and your friend? Are we church?'

'Of course,' I replied, 'there is us, and Jesus is here in the middle of us. I expect he would love to have a cake.'

'Is it all right to say this,' queried the reporter sternly, 'that Jesus would like to have a cake?'

'It is not a flippant comment,' I replied, 'if you read the gospels you will see that Jesus loved to eat with his friends, and that many important things happened on these occasions. Nothing has changed. On this very day a meal between Christian brothers and sisters is not just a very pleasurable thing to do, but also a form of sacrament. Of course Jesus would love to take a sandwich and a cup of tea with us.'

He looked unconvinced. I continued.

'In the book of Revelation, what does Jesus say he will do if we open the door when he knocks?'

'He will come in.'

'And what will he do with us?'

'Err ...'

'He will *eat* with us.'

'Hmm.' He frowned, looking as if he might be on the point of bursting, even though he had only sipped his tea and nibbled at a cake.

I had to leave it there. I did my best, but Jesus was absolutely right. Getting new wine into old wineskins is a heck of a business.

14

Pronouncement about the Sabbath

2 : 23 – 28

One Sabbath he was going through the grain fields; and as they made their way his disciples began to pluck heads of grain.

The Pharisees said to him, 'Look, why are they doing what is not lawful on the Sabbath?'

And he said to them, 'Have you never read what David did when he and his companions were hungry and in need of food? He entered the house of God, when Abiathar was high priest, and ate the bread of the Presence, which it is not lawful for any but the priests to eat, and he gave some to his companions.'

Then he said to them, 'The Sabbath was made for humankind, and not humankind for the Sabbath; so the Son of Man is lord even of the Sabbath.'

I USED TO KNOW A MAN WHO ENRAGED AND FRUSTRATED HIS family by postponing the moment when he opened birthday or Christmas presents for days or even weeks after the event. It drove his wife and children wild. Quite late in life, as a result of what one might call therapeutic prayer sessions, he discovered the reason for this strange behaviour. A hidden memory surfaced. As a small boy he had always wanted a watch. One Christmas his mother, a strange, rather cruel person, promised him his wish would be granted. However, on Christmas morning she flew into a rage with her small son for some trivial reason and threw the brightly wrapped present in his direction. It missed him but hit the wall and fell to the floor. When he finally unwrapped his gift he found that the watch had been smashed to pieces. Sounds too neat to be true, doesn't it? But that is what happened, and that is why he had become so reluctant to open presents as an adult.

I am not quite so bad as that, but in the past (have you noticed that Christian speakers and writers only ever have problems in the past?) I have had a tendency to *enshrine* my presents instead of using and enjoying them. Why? I'm not sure, except that the dread of decay and ultimate failure has always been an obstacle-like part of my life-view that I have needed to steer around at important moments. Until recently, I had a drawer upstairs into which I would place gifts once I had unwrapped them. There in the darkness they would sit, uncorrupted and unused until the indignant protests of the givers forced me into getting them out and *doing* something with them.

I don't know if God gets as annoyed over our misuse of the Sabbath as my children did over me stowing their gifts away in my drawer, but the principle is exactly the same, and I suspect that the same sort of thing has happened with the Bible. The Pharisees, then and now, have enshrined a gift from God that was supposed to be *used*, not only for praise and worship, but for refreshment and relaxation after a long week. They have turned it into a thing whose nature is not far removed from that of an idol. How silly! Come on, all you followers of Jesus, let's get this and all of God's other good and practical gifts out of the drawer and make him happy by enjoying them.

The Man with
a Withered Hand

3 : 1 – 6

Again he entered the synagogue, and a man was there who had a
withered hand. They watched him to see whether he would cure
him on the Sabbath, so that they might accuse him.

And he said to the man who had the withered hand, 'Come
forward.' Then he said to them, 'Is it lawful to do good or to do
harm on the Sabbath, to save life or to kill?'

But they were silent. He looked around at them with anger; he
was grieved at their hardness of heart and said to the man, 'Stretch
out your hand.' He stretched it out, and his hand was restored. The
Pharisees went out and immediately conspired with the Herodians
against him, how to destroy him.

P EOPLE REALLY HATE JESUS, DON'T THEY?'

Thus spoke a friend of mine, wearied by the task of being a
Christian in everyday life, as we relaxed together over coffee
and biscuits.

'What do you mean?'

'Well,' he sighed and dunked a biscuit, 'with some people it's
not just that they don't want to know, it's as if the very thought
of him starts up a sort of boiling rage in them. The sound of his
name almost makes them sick. Why do you think that is?'

I searched for answers to offer my friend, because I agreed
with him, but I don't think any of my suggestions were very
convincing. We agreed that, in recent years, there had been
some extremely unfortunate representations of the Christian
faith in the media. That was probably very relevant, but there
had to be more to it than that.

Now, as I read this familiar tale, a new idea strikes me. These Pharisees had double-padlocked their minds against the intrusion of any new ideas about who Jesus might be or the significance of the things he was saying and doing. It wouldn't matter how much sense he talked, or how many people were raised from the dead, or healed like this man with the withered arm, because the attitude of the Pharisees towards Jesus was unswervingly hostile and their ultimate aim was his destruction.

Why?

I think the fundamental reply to that question might also be the clue that my friend and I were looking for. The answer is that he wanted their whole lives, as he still wants the whole lives of men and women in this age. He wants them to step out of the protective shell formed by religion or sin or activities and follow him in that vulnerable state. Following Jesus is not a hobby, or a pastime, or engagement in uncommitted discussion, or an area of study, or a moral code, or membership of a club, or going to church, or any of the other commendable but purely human varieties of involvement that we could list. I believe that those Pharisees had something in common with an enormous number of people in the present day, namely, a deep and usually unconscious awareness that following Jesus is, in one sense at least, like entering the door of an alien spaceship. When it takes off we will have no control over our destinies, no clear idea of where we are going, and no option of returning. Either we trust the captain of the ship or we don't go.

The Pharisees saw a strange bright light. They felt the ground trembling beneath their feet and they were afraid for their lives. They didn't want to go.

They were right to be afraid.

They were wrong not to go.

16

A Multitude
at the Seaside

3 : 7 – 12

Jesus departed with his disciples to the sea, and a great multitude from Galilee followed him; hearing all that he was doing, they came to him in great numbers from Judea, Jerusalem, Idumea, beyond the Jordan, and the region around Tyre and Sidon. He told his disciples to have a boat ready for him because of the crowd, so that they would not crush him; for he had cured many, so that all who had diseases pressed upon him to touch him. Whenever the unclean spirits saw him, they fell down before him and shouted, 'You are the Son of God!' But he sternly ordered them not to make him known.

CRUSH HIM? CRUSH JESUS? HOW COULD THERE BE ANY suggestion that the Son of God would have to put up with being crushed by the crowd? Surely, all it required was one spiritual flick of the wrist and troublesome bodies would go flying through the air like those dispensable baddies in Bruce Lee movies. If he could heal people and stop fig trees from growing and turn water into wine, why on earth would there be any problem about simple crowd control? What was going on? What accounts for these apparently arbitrary page-breaks that are inserted between the natural and the supernatural in the lives of Jesus and his followers?

Asking this question opens a whole can of biblical worms, doesn't it? Why was it necessary that *anything* unpleasant should happen? Why was Herod allowed to kill all those little children? Why did Joseph and Mary have to go sneaking round the middle east with the baby Jesus to avoid being found? Why did John the Baptist have to be beheaded? Why did Stephen have to be stoned to death? Why did Paul have to be cold and naked and starved and shipwrecked and stoned and beaten and imprisoned and allowed no relief from the thorns in his flesh, whatever they might have been? Why, if it comes to that, did Jesus have to be beaten up and humiliated and crucified? Why, we might as well ask, did God create the world in the first place when he knew full well that we were going to fail and it was all going to go so very wrong? Why does he use his power in some situations and withhold it in others?

If I was able to devise a set of simple answers to these questions I would have a massive bestseller on my hands. But I am not able to do that, not even for publishers as amiable and generous as mine. Sorry, fellers! These are problems that I cannot solve. I simply do not know.

Of course, you can find answers. Some who are reading this will be itching to offer them to me. People have written whole books that include arguments aimed at explaining these anomalies. I know most of those arguments. I used to employ some of them myself when I was forced into a corner. Nowadays, I find them interesting, ingenious and generally unconvincing. I have no intention of repeating them here. Let me say these things, though, and, as far as I am concerned, they apply to all the hard questions in the Christian faith.

First, I am always happy to explain my beliefs and to answer any questions that I am capable of answering.

Secondly, when I am not capable of providing an answer I am much happier in my not-knowing than I ever was in my thin justifications.

Third, the centre of my faith is Jesus. Knowing him is the source from which all other things spring. I trust him with unanswerable questions because that is as nothing compared to trusting him with my soul.

Fourth, if you feel you are drowning in these kinds of questions, you might like to turn to the fourth chapter of John's gospel and pick up the passion and urgency with which Jesus speaks of his desire for a harvest of souls. You may feel, having read those words, that the questions and answers can wait.

Finally, apart from all these other considerations, the single fact that Jesus was concerned about being crushed is sufficient to combat the silly contention that God will protect us physically in all circumstances.

It is a rich cake, this faith of ours. Let's be positive. Better to enjoy its richness than to pull out odd currants and sit staring at them, worrying that they might be dead flies.

17

Jesus Appoints the Twelve

3 : 13 – 19

He went up the mountain and called to him those whom he wanted, and they came to him. And he appointed twelve, whom he also named apostles, to be with him, and to be sent out to proclaim the message, and to have authority to cast out demons. So he appointed the twelve: Simon (to whom he gave the name Peter); James son of Zebedee and John the brother of James (to whom he gave the name Boanerges, that is, Sons of Thunder); and Andrew, and Philip, and Bartholomew, and Matthew, and Thomas, and James son of Alphaeus, and Thaddaeus, and Simon the Cananaean, and Judas Iscariot, who betrayed him.

HERE, IN THIS GROUP OF APOSTLES (A WORD WHICH I AM told means 'men who are sent out') we have, among others, a zealot, an ex-tax collector, two Greek sounding fellows, two bad-tempered brothers, the loyal, stubborn Simon Peter, Judas, who was later to betray Jesus and four others. They were a disparate bunch, and, as far as we know, they had just one thing in common – they had been called to follow Jesus.

Ring any bells?

A few years ago, when we attended a church in the Midlands, I realised to my horror one day that I was building up a real head of steam about a pair of my fellow-worshippers, two older men who usually sat near to me during services. Why? I am ashamed to say that it was because their singing voices were loud, raucous, untuneful and oppressively enthusiastic. Once these two really got going, particularly in such beautiful hymns as the one that is sung to the tune of 'Danny Boy', I tended to stop singing altogether. It was like trying to swim in a log-jam. I felt *so* irritable! I thought bad, harsh things about them. I indulged fantasies about whipping them to death with service sheets or making them eat entire church Bibles. I had to repent in the end. Who did I think I was? Why shouldn't my two brothers have a great time singing their hearts out to God on a Sunday morning?

'*Because it sounds so horrible!*' a small and unrepentant part of me continued to whimperingly protest.

I do laugh at myself now, but it is a little alarming, isn't it? For a short time I was in real trouble over this trivial issue. How will I survive when more serious differences occur between myself and others who have been called in exactly the same way by exactly the same master?

18

Jesus and Beelzebul

3 : 20 – 30

Then he went home; and the crowd came together again, so that they could not even eat. When his family heard it, they went out to restrain him, for people were saying, 'He has gone out of his mind.'

And the scribes who came down from Jerusalem said, 'He has Beelzebul, and by the ruler of the demons he casts out demons.'

And he called them to him, and spoke to them in parables, 'How can Satan cast out Satan? If a kingdom is divided against itself, that kingdom cannot stand. And if a house is divided against itself, that house will not be able to stand. And if Satan has risen up against himself and is divided, he cannot stand, but his end has come. But no one can enter a strong man's house and plunder his property without first tying up the strong man; then indeed the house can be plundered.

'Truly I tell you, people will be forgiven for their sins and whatever blasphemies they utter; but whoever blasphemes against the Holy Spirit can never have forgiveness, but is guilty of an eternal sin' – for they had said, 'He has an unclean spirit.'

WHAT A MOMENT! THE MESSIAH, THE HOLY ONE OF GOD, God himself, he who was shortly to voluntarily die for the salvation of millions of men and women is accused of representing the source of all evil. If the instant when Jesus heard these accusations was ever to be portrayed on the West End stage there would have to be a highly dramatic, thunderous roll of drums accompanied by flashes of lightning and possibly some sort of mighty rushing wind effect. It would be good on stage.

Poor Jesus was truly man and truly God. Even on a normal human level this sort of false accusation can take your breath away. Might not the enraged, truly-man part of him have been tempted to grab one of these mouthy scribes, fling him to the ground, sit on his chest, bang his head rhythmically on the gravel and make a few salient points through clenched teeth?

'How *dare* you! How *dare* you even *suggest* that I have a demon! How can you *possibly* bring yourself to be so wilfully obtuse! You *silly – silly – silly* little scribe! Take *that*! And *that*! And *that*!'

Of course, he did not respond in such a wild way. Clearing the temple (an event we shall read about in a later chapter), was a considered and deliberate act of righteous aggression, but there is no room for uncontrolled violence in the Kingdom of God. Instead, Jesus delivered a much more dignified and damning response to what had been said, concluding with his chilling assertion that forgiveness would never be available for those who abused the Holy Spirit as these men had done. I can't help wondering how much sleep those scribes got that night, or any other night for that matter.

This issue of the duality of Jesus' nature, one I have already touched on, is highly relevant to those of us who call ourselves Christians, simply because we are in exactly the same position. Leaving aside the glaringly obvious differences between the Son of God and you and I, we are real human beings struggling with a real and difficult world, just as he is revealed to have been in this gospel, and the Holy Spirit inhabits us, just as it inhabited him. This undeniable fact has, or ought to have, a profound effect on the choices we make in all sorts of situations. I have given in to more worldly impulses (the scribe head-banging sort of option) far too often, but there was one occasion when the good counsel of the Holy Spirit prevailed.

We were on holiday in the beautiful county of Cornwall with friends. One evening we went to an open-air theatre presentation in a superb setting on a cliff overlooking the sea. By the time we left it was getting dark. As Bridget threaded our car in reverse between other vehicles, trying to get out of the crowded car-park, she caught the corner of another car, damaging one of its brake-lights. The owner of the damaged car was nowhere to be seen. After waiting for a decent interval, we decided to wedge a note under the windscreen wiper, giving our address, explaining what had happened and promising to pay for repairs as soon as we received a copy of the bill.

Sure enough, a bill duly appeared, accompanied by a letter expressing gratitude for Bridget's honesty in admitting blame for the minor collision. Our finances fluctuate wildly, and it was a few days before we were able to write a cheque that would definitely not do a kangaroo impression. It was, in fact, as I was sitting down to write this cheque that a further letter arrived from the lady whose car had been damaged. It was a very angry letter. It was a *very* angry letter.

The money had not arrived. *Why* had the money not arrived? Why was she still waiting for money to cover an accident that was, after all, not *her* fault?

There was more in the same vein. It filled me with fury. It made me hiss through my teeth. I felt like jumping up and down and shaking my fists. I composed long sarcastic letters in my head and imagined her reading them.

'Do you not realise,' I raved hypothetically, 'that if my wife had not left a note under your stupid windscreen you would never have known who did it, and you would never have received a stupid penny to cover the repair of your stupid little brake-light? Has it really not occurred to you that you are only able to take this stupidly high moral tone because we were good and humble and Christian enough to prostrate ourselves in penitence before you?'

Oh, yes, my fantasy letters would have shown that woman the love of God, and no mistake!

'What would be the very best way?' a little voice queried in the back of my mind. 'What would be the very best way for this lady who is probably not a follower of Jesus. For all you know this may be one of the very few contacts with Christians that she has had or is likely to have in the whole of her life. What is the best way?'

Sighing a little, I wrote the cheque, and enclosed a note apologising for its late arrival. I admitted that I had felt hurt by the anger in her letter, but expressed a hope that she would be conscious of our good intentions. I injected as much warmth into the letter as I could, and by the time the words were on the paper I was beginning to mean them. I also enclosed a copy of one of my books (why should she escape with no punishment at all?) dedicated to her on the title-page. In return she sent me a most gracious and apologetic letter. I was so glad that I had mentally screwed up all those hypothetical letters and thrown them into the hypothetical bin.

The way of the Spirit is always the best way, but, oh my goodness – isn't it hard sometimes?

19

The True Kindred of Jesus

3 : 31 – 35

Then his mother and his brothers came; and standing outside, they sent to him and called him. A crowd was sitting around him; and they said to him, 'Your mother and your brothers and sisters are outside, asking for you.'

And he replied, 'Who are my mother and my brothers?' And looking at those who sat around him, he said, 'Here are my mother and my brothers! Whoever does the will of God is my brother and sister and mother.'

M Y WIFE AND I HAVE DIFFERING OPINIONS ON THE STATE of Mary's mind when she and her sons arrived to collect their singular relative. The fact that neither of us will know the actual truth until we meet Mary does not prevent us from expressing our opposing views with all the vehemence and freedom that long-married couples are privileged to bring to their 'discussions'.

Bridget points to the suggestion, a few verses earlier, that his family, meaning his mother and brothers, had come to rescue him from making an even greater idiot of himself than he was already doing. Even Mary, Bridget contends, must have reached the point by now where she was seriously concerned that her son had flipped his lid in a frighteningly self-destructive way. His brothers quite definitely felt like that. In the seventh chapter of John's gospel we are told simply that 'even his own brothers did not believe in him'.

Okay, his brothers thought he was off his head. But his mother? Mary? This is the woman who had been visited and spoken to by an angel. She had conceived by some strange power of the Holy Spirit. She had heard Elizabeth's account of the prediction of John's birth and ministry, and seen the baby jump in her elderly relative's womb. She had seen the shepherds and the wise men come to worship her baby and bring gifts, as though to a king. She had seen how, through dreams and warnings, God had protected the young child from Herod's wrath. She had lost the twelve-year-old Jesus for three days in Jerusalem at the time of Passover, and discovered him at last, amazing teachers in the temple with his understanding and his replies to their questions. She had watched as a much older Jesus turned water to wine at the wedding in Cana. She must have witnessed hundreds of healings. And these are only the things that happened to be recorded. There will have been many, many more. She had lived with and loved the Son of God for more than thirty years, and she knew, because she had been told, that a sword would one day pierce her heart.

I don't think she thought he was mad. But I do think that by now the pain in her heart had become severe.

And Jesus? What of him? Does he look out across and over the heads of the crowd as they absorb his important piece of teaching on relationships in the Kingdom of God, and catch his mother's eye. There she stands in front of her concerned, embarrassed sons, her expression warm, worried and willing as ever, one of the small number of people in his life, perhaps, who would continue to love him with the same unconditional love if, in the end, his brothers were to be proved right, and he should turn out to be nothing but the tragically deluded son of a Galilean carpenter.

'Dear woman.'

Those are the words, recorded in John's gospel, with which Jesus would one day address Mary from the cross.

'Dear woman.'

20

The Parable of the Sower

4 : 1 – 9

Again he began to teach beside the sea. Such a very large crowd gathered around him that he got into a boat on the sea and sat there, while the whole crowd was beside the sea on the land. He began to teach them many things in parables, and in his teaching he said to them: 'Listen! A sower went out to sow. And as he sowed, some seed fell on the path, and the birds came and ate it up. Other seed fell on rocky ground, where it did not have much soil, and it sprang up quickly, since it had no depth of soil. And when the sun rose, it was scorched; and since it had no root, it withered away. Other seed fell among thorns, and the thorns grew up and choked it, and it yielded no grain. Other seed fell into good soil and brought forth grain, growing up and increasing and yielding thirty and sixty and a hundredfold.' And he said, 'Let anyone with ears to hear listen!'

As I WRITE THIS BOOK I AM IN THE MIDDLE OF YET ANOTHER scheme designed to increase my fitness. This latest ploy involves a bicycle, given to me by my wife as a birthday present (no, this time I didn't put it into my drawer and forget about it – it was too big or I might have), and so far it has all been very enjoyable. The boy with the bike is reborn – yet again – and his new bike has fifteen gears! Yippee! Almost every day I cycle from Hailsham to Polegate along the Cuckoo Trail, a local footpath resurrected from one of those railway branch-lines that were crucified back in the sixties by nasty Pontius Beeching, the transport minister of the day. This regular exercise makes me feel physically better, and it also gives me a chance to mentally pursue essential inner dialogues about the work I'm trying to do.

Quite apart from anything else it's a lovely route to follow, with a green (turning to red and brown and gold at the moment) feast of fields and trees to left and right for almost the whole distance. I always stop at the same place before turning to begin the return journey. Just off the main footpath there is an idyllic little corner where you can prop your bike up, gaze across two or three fields and see the South Downs rising gently in the distance.

Yesterday, with a sort of casserole of bits of this book simmering gently on the back-burner of my mind, I noted that the new crop in the field just over the fence was starting to make the pattern of its planting very clear. The field of healthy emerald shoots stretched away endlessly in parallel lines, some gently curving and some straight, a much more mechanical arrangement than in Jesus' time no doubt, but probably very similar in most other ways.

I noticed something else, and it suggested one more category that needs to be added to this parable. (Incidentally, if that worries you, there's no need to be concerned, because I asked God about it and he said it was fine.) I noticed prints from the tyres of machines that had been used for planting or spraying or whatever other processes the farmer had deemed necessary for the future welfare of his crop. They were very broad and very widespread and wherever they occurred, the crop didn't. Now, I feel quite sure that Jesus never trampled any of his delicate little seedlings out of existence, but I am equally sure that some of his followers have been far less careful. When God has been busy planting seeds it really is important that we give them space and time to grow, rather than trampling all over them with our worldly or religious concerns, or pulling up the odd one or two to see if the roots are getting any longer. Remember the parable of the wheat and the tares in the thirteenth chapter of Matthew's gospel?

'Shall we pull out the weeds?' ask the servants.

'No,' replies the master, 'because while you are pulling the weeds, you may root up the wheat with them.'

'Besides which,' he might have added, 'if you go clumping around the fields in your great big size-twelve sandals, you're likely to squash as many as you save ...'

21

The Purpose of the Parables

4 : 10 – 20

When he was alone, those who were around him along with the twelve asked him about the parables. And he said to them, 'To you has been given the secret of the kingdom of God, but for those outside, everything comes in parables; in order that "they may indeed look, but not perceive, and may indeed listen, but not understand; so that they may not turn again and be forgiven."'

And he said to them, 'Do you not understand this parable? Then how will you understand all the parables? The sower sows the word. These are the ones on the path where the word is sown: when they hear, Satan immediately comes and takes away the word that is sown in them. And these are the ones sown on rocky ground: when they hear the word, they immediately receive it with joy. But they have no root, and endure only for a while; then, when trouble or persecution arises on account of the word, immediately they fall away. And others are those sown among the thorns: these are the ones who hear the word, but the cares of the world, and the lure of wealth, and the desire for other things come in and choke the word, and it yields nothing. And these are the ones sown on the good soil: they hear the word and accept it and bear fruit, thirty and sixty and a hundredfold.'

As we all know, time becomes fluid and meaningless in the context of eternity. Bearing that in mind, you will not be terribly surprised to hear that the plans for Jesus' ministry and parables were actually submitted to a joint committee of leading Christian organisations and church leaders in the twenty-first century before he set out on his journey of birth, ministry, crucifixion and resurrection. I have managed to obtain copies of the reports issued by this committee. Here is the first part, the one concerning parables.

Dear Sir,

Thank you for submitting your parables and your three-year plan for ministry to the committee. We have examined your proposals with the greatest care and interest. The following is a summary of our responses to your suggestions. I shall deal with the parables first.

You write in an economic and entertaining manner, and you clearly mean well, but, as a general point, the committee feels you might need to give some thought to the nature of your potential audience and the fact that the ends do not always justify the means.

Your stories include episodes of torture, robbery, cruelty, murder, extreme violence, death, jealousy, lies, hypocrisy and gratuitous insults to respected members of the community. In the scene involving the rich man and Lazarus, regrettably you have found it necessary to include what one of our longest standing committee members has described as an 'utterly disgusting' reference to dogs licking the sores of the beggar as he lay beside the rich man's gate. Would you not agree that such a general abundance of negative content, and such an explicit reference as this latter one, are more likely to repel than to attract? A little indulgent on your part? Some of us did wonder. May I respectfully suggest that you examine yourself to see if these elements are included for reasons of your own that have no basis in responsible ministry. Try to be honest. We feel sure you will agree that any serious intention to draw people into the Christian faith is unlikely to succeed through the use of offensive or overly-dramatic images and events.

One or two of the stories I am afraid we have had to exclude altogether. In our view the tale of the Prodigal Son, for instance, fails on all levels, and, I am sorry to say, dangerously distorts the nature of God. Your depiction of the prodigal's father is sentimental, wildly optimistic, and, frankly, likely to inspire less rather than more respect for God in your listeners. We would all love to believe that things are as you describe them, but the truth is the truth, and we shall not be set free by a pleasant fiction. I suspect you are actually fully aware that our cause will be poorly served by such a diluted account of the realities of repentance, commitment, and the awesome power of God. Drastic rewriting might help, but to be honest the result would be a different story altogether.

The committee as a whole felt that the tale of the Good Samaritan shows distinct promise, but needs rescuing from the twin dangers of sensationalism and crude criticism of those who, let us face it, have little or no right of reply. We must constantly remind ourselves that we are representing God in all that we do and say. One of our members has kindly undertaken to adjust this parable as an example and encouragement to you of what might be done in the future. His carefully balanced, much more concise, and, in its own way, more hard-hitting version reads as follows:

'A man was going down from Jerusalem to Jericho, when he realised that he had developed quite a severe cold, and was completely without medicines or tissues. A priest and a Levite, both of them busily and legitimately caught up in their own very worthwhile activities, failed to notice this need as they passed by on their way to minister to others, whereas a Samaritan, perhaps less burdened with responsibilities and therefore able to respond with greater sensitivity, supplied the assistance required. Thus we see that even a Samaritan may take his turn at being a neighbour to another, but let us thank God for priests, Levites *and* Samaritans.'

Other contributions from committee members included suggestions for improvements in, among others, the parable of the Tenants. Why, many of us asked, do you seem so very intent on shocking those who will be looking to you for a message of love and peace? When the first servant is sent to collect his master's fruit we would like to see him treated in a less than friendly fashion instead of being beaten, the second one being spoken to quite brusquely rather than being killed, the third servant rudely ignored as opposed to being stoned, and the landowner's son subjected to remarks that are positively offensive instead of being robbed of his inheritance and murdered.

Do you begin to see how easy it is to make exactly the same point, but without recourse to ugly and unhelpful imagery? The Christian faith has no need to rely on worldly methods for communication of its truths and principles. If you will accept a gentle word from an old hand, it may be, you know, that you are simply trying too hard.

I have included reports and comments on all of your attempts at storytelling, but I would like to make specific mention of just one other parable. I fear that your story of The Sower caused considerable disquiet among most of the members of our committee, as it undoubtedly would among a wider audience. Allow me to say that you really *must* maintain strict awareness of the fact that your message will not be for one era only. In the nineteenth, twentieth and twenty-first centuries, for instance, determinism will be a dominant influence on general perceptions of responsibility, motivation and blame. The imagery you employ in this parable is quite well worked out and fairly picturesque in its own way, but let me ask you this. Are you confident that the God it projects will be considered just? I shall use your own metaphor. Did the path *ask* to be a path? Could the rocky ground *help* being rocky ground? Did the thorns do anything whatsoever to *deserve* being thorns? You and we know the answers to these questions, do we not? Our God is not a God of injustice and unequal treatment. Do think on these things.

There is a great deal of work to be done on these parables of yours. But be encouraged. The committee commends your hard work and sees the seeds of something quite useful if you will apply yourself to the sorts of adaptation that we are recommending. Do send us more stories if you wish.

22

A Lamp under a Bushel Basket

4 : 21 – 25

He said to them, 'Is a lamp brought in to be put under the bushel basket, or under the bed, and not on the lamp stand? For there is nothing hidden, except to be disclosed; nor is anything secret, except to come to light. Let anyone with ears to hear listen!'

And he said to them, 'Pay attention to what you hear; the measure you give will be the measure you get, and still more will be given you. For to those who have, more will be given; and from those who have nothing, even what they have will be taken away.'

THERE WAS CONSIDERABLE UNCERTAINTY ABOUT THE OPENING words of this passage in the church youth group that I used to belong to. Having gloomily gathered the sadly distorted idea that, by a rather grumpy effort of the will, God loved us despite the fact that we were miserable lumps of inchoate uselessness, it seemed very vain to even think about displaying our spiritual light, even if it was as dim as a Toc H lamp.

The thing we were forgetting, of course, is that the normal function of a torch or a lamp is not to draw attention to itself, but to allow areas that were previously in darkness to be revealed. It is, for instance, in the light of another person's kindness and generosity that we might begin to see how our own attitudes to other people fall short of the mark. That is a most valuable and uncomfortable experience and it has happened to me more than once. And, of course, there are degrees of revelation. A very tiny lamp might only shed a very tiny amount of light, but it may be all that is needed.

Sometimes these human lights reveal the source of their own

power. I once gave a talk in a large church at Clifton, near Bristol. As I was heading for the bookstall at the beginning of the interval I was met in the centre aisle by an elderly lady who was just about managing to drag herself along with the aid of two sticks. Stopping and clutching my arm, she looked straight into my face and said, 'We've got a *wonderful* Lord, haven't we?'

In itself, that sentence of hers was a neutral one, wasn't it? After all, it might have been expressed so insincerely that it cast shadows instead of spreading light. It could have been nothing more than mechanical repetition, the sort of religious loop recording that continues its hollow broadcast without ever having to actually mean anything.

This time it was not like that. It is difficult to describe the impact of this lady's words on me. All I can tell you is that my memory of the incident is full of light. Her face was filled with light. The very air around her seemed to shine. It was as though a bright stream issued from her and was continually replenished in her. She shone with Jesus, and my feeble spirit was strengthened and blessed beyond words.

This principle of giving and being replenished, exemplified by that radiant lady, and described here by Jesus, is one of the very basic tenets of the Christian faith. It applies to time and money and generosity and care and listening and giving and giving up and sacrifice and a host of other things. I must give and give and give to ensure that there will always be a space available to receive more from God, so that yet more may be given.

Let the rivers flow and keep them flowing. There are no droughts in the Kingdom of heaven.

5

The Parable
of the Growing Seed

4 : 26 – 29

He also said, 'The kingdom of God is as if someone would scatter seed on the ground, and would sleep and rise night and day, and the seed would sprout and grow, he does not know how. The earth produces of itself, first the stalk, then the head, then the full grain in the head. But when the grain is ripe, at once he goes in with his sickle, because the harvest has come.'

ALL THIS HAS HAPPENED. WHEN JESUS SAYS THE HARVEST has come, he is speaking of the moment in which you read these words, just as certainly as he is talking about the moment when I write them. The grain is ripe and ready, and, as Jesus points out in the fourth chapter of John's gospel, there really are very few workers around to bring it in. We shall each be allotted a different role in the gathering process, but the needs of the Kingdom are great. We cannot afford our number to be reduced by one, as it will be if either you or I lose our nerve and opt out of the task. One day, quite suddenly, all this stale old religious stuff is going to mean something dreadful and wonderful to the lost and the saved. The full grain is in the head, but a very cold winter is coming. We must try to be brave.

The Parable of the Mustard Seed

4 : 30 – 32

He also said, 'With what can we compare the kingdom of God, or what parable will we use for it? It is like a mustard seed, which, when sown upon the ground, is the smallest of all the seeds on earth; yet when it is sown it grows up and becomes the greatest of all shrubs, and puts forth large branches, so that the birds of the air can make nests in its shade.'

WHEN MY FAITH WAVERS AND I BEGIN TO ASK MYSELF ghastly questions about oblivion and the dull worthlessness of plodding ever onward towards death (my spiritual Eeyore mode), one of the things that revives me is a walk in the country. Not just because the Sussex countryside is beautiful, although it is, but because in the course of walking just a few miles I am likely to pass or catch a glimpse of three or four village churches. Viewing these sweetly pachydermatous structures has a very soothing effect on me. Twenty centuries ago, in an age when communication was basic in the extreme, one self-effacing man in an obscure corner of the world said and did some things over the course of three short years that resulted in there being one or more churches in every hamlet, village, town and city, over four thousand altogether in Great Britain alone. Staggering!

And, of course, that is but a small part of it. I have made a nest in the shade of the tree that grew from the mustard seed of the life, death and resurrection of Jesus, and I am only one of billions.

While we are on the subject, I recently discovered some mustard seeds that were planted a very long time ago. Perhaps because of lack of exposure to light they had done almost no growing at all. Now, though, they have been replanted, and are likely to produce a harvest that I could never have imagined.

It is not an easy thing for me to write about.

Those of you who have been bribed or threatened into reading my books in the past may be aware that my relationship with my father left a lot to be desired. He was a Roman Catholic convert, a man who wanted his faith to affect and impinge upon the way in which he dealt with his life. In the main he was disappointed in this desire. He was a possessive, obsessional, tortured individual, who had everything that he wanted, but, because of a profound lack of self-esteem, was incapable of enjoying it. The area of my mind occupied by his memory has been a dark and unhappy place for the whole of my life. Just a few weeks ago, a little light entered that darkness, and these three mustard seeds began to grow.

I was looking through some of the things in my study, trying to decide which old items of rubbish could be thrown away in order to make room for new items of rubbish. Slipped inside the cover of a book that I hadn't looked at for years and years, I found a letter. It was a letter written to me by my father when I was about nineteen years old and a student at theatre school in Bristol. I am almost sure that it is the only letter he ever sent me, and it was a reply to the only letter that I ever sent him. Shortly after leaving home to go to college in Bristol I wrote my father the kind of letter that I thought he would really want to read. I don't know how sincere it was, but it thanked him for all he had done for me and expressed a degree of affection that I could never have put into spoken words.

His reply was friendly without being effusive, offering advice on practical matters and not reacting in any specific way to the sentiments I had expressed in my letter to him. I remembered how disappointed I had been by this reply. There was no exchange of feeling. I was very naïve all those years ago. I had barely glanced at the end of the letter. Now, as I looked more carefully at the very bottom of the final page, I realised that I had been wrong. My father had indeed found a way to pass on more important feelings. Immediately after the signature there were three kisses. Mustard seeds.

25

The Use of Parables

4 : 33 – 34

With many such parables he spoke the word to them, as they were able to hear it; he did not speak to them except in parables, but he explained everything in private to his disciples.

HERE IN THESE TWO VERSES WE DISCOVER A COLLECTION OF words that should, in my not very humble opinion, be displayed on the bathroom mirror and screen-saver and filofax cover of every man or woman who has any intention of talking to people about the things of God. Jesus spoke to the people in nothing but parables. In parables only did he speak to the people. The people heard only parables from Jesus. Parables alone did the people hear from Jesus. Are you getting tired of me saying that? I repeat it in all its permutations because some of us may still be missing the point.

Jesus might have had a variety of motives for approaching his ministry in this way, but there was one overwhelming reason for using stories. No prizes for guessing. People liked stories. They enjoyed listening to stories. They were likely to remember the content and point of stories. Indeed, so entertained, absorbed and fascinated were they by some of these stories that, on at least two occasions, thousands of them forgot all about the need to organise lunch and ended up sitting on a hillside feeling hungry (fortunately for them, Jesus was as sensitive to physical requirements as he was to spiritual need).

How have we managed to lose sight of the fact that, in this respect, people do not and probably never will change? Somewhere on the long, strangely winding road between the years when Jesus walked the Earth and the present day, a view must have developed in some quarters that the content of preaching and teaching should be more or less on a par with nasty medicine. You don't like it, but you've got to take it and swallow it for your own good. It doesn't matter if it's boring as long as it's worthy. Dull acquiescence to an hour and a half of grey, turgid, incontrovertible truth is just what you need to keep your faith fizzing along.

I ask you! What possible merit can there be in an irksome and unvarying diet of thick porridge without salt or sweetness, that will just about keep you alive but make you wish you weren't? Please don't misunderstand me, by the way. Not for one moment am I suggesting that people should not be challenged and made to face up to hard truths. Many of the parables that Jesus told had exactly that effect on those who heard them. Imagine it.

'So, who is my neighbour?' asks an expert on the law, hoping to catch the master out.

'Well,' says Jesus, 'a certain man was going down from Jerusalem to Jericho ...'

The story of violence and neglect and compassion that we know so well begins and continues. Soon the expert is so engrossed that his original question has flown from his grown-up head like a migrating bird. He is a child listening to a tale.

'So,' says Jesus as the story ends, 'which of these three do you think was a neighbour to the man who fell into the hands of robbers?'

'The one who had mercy on him, of course.'

It was a prompt reply. But after that? Did the expert on the law experience something of an inner shock as it dawned on him that the outcome of the verbal three-card trick he had just witnessed was more revealing of himself than of Jesus?

No, the technique of teaching through stories certainly doesn't let anyone off the hook. Quite often parables entertain us at the front door while the truth creeps in through a side-window and sandbags us on the back of the head.

There are some first-class storytellers around, but we need more. Let's pray that more will arise. Let's encourage them. Let's be them. Let's not be boring. Let's not put up with being bored.

It is also worth mentioning that parables are by no means limited to stories told by public speakers. If we look out for them we may well spot parables in our own daily experiences, events or situations that contain within them a message or signpost for the direction of our lives.

Here is a rather obvious one from my own life.

It happened when I had spent most of one week in a place overflowing with passion and high drama, a place where one was able to witness starbursts of joy and floods of tears. It was a place where dreams were being fulfilled and hearts were being broken, where one could see the best and the worst of what it means to be human. I had seen scorn and encouragement, compassion and vindictiveness, bitterness and courage, optimism and the final demise of hope.

What place was this where tragedy battled with delight? Perhaps some sad, war-torn corner of a distant land, where unsung heroes battled hideous giants of callousness and exploitation?

No, it was the local Dance Festival in which my thirteen year old daughter was taking part. I don't know if you are familiar with events like this, but if you are, and you have endured them, I know you will have no wish to read on. To have such memories stirred would depress you, so do feel free to move on to the next bit of this book. We'll catch you up in a minute.

For those who have never experienced the above phenomenon, I'll try to explain.

You are in a large hall or theatre with a wide stage at one end. In the centre aisle of the auditorium, close to the stage, stands a raised dais on which two chairs and a table have been placed. This is where the adjudicator and her assistant sit in order to have a good view of the performances. The adjudicator is responsible for awarding a mark to each child in each class.

There are many classes. They include Modern, Tap, Ballet, Greek, Song and Dance, National, Improvisation and other categories that have been blessedly wiped from my memory. The number of children appearing in each class varies. Two of the ones I had to sit through in the course of that week seemed to involve several hundred children and take several days to complete, but that may not have been an entirely reliable or sane judgement.

One of the things that produced such warped assessments was the fact that a bewilderingly high number of these solo dances appeared to be identical. The titles were different. In fact, now that I think about it, the titles were the *most* different thing about them.

In the Character class that I watched for a month or two on one of the days, for instance, the monotonous, amplified voice from behind the curtain announced, 'Mary Jones, dancing The River. The river flows from the mountains down to the sea.'

This was the cue for Mary Jones to appear on stage, where she hopped about and ran around for a bit being a river flowing down to the sea.

'Next,' declared the dispassionate amplified voice, 'Nicola Edwards, dancing The Shepherdess. The girl who tends the flock belonging to her master goes off to search for a lost lamb, and returns only to find that a wolf is attacking the rest of the flock. She fights off the wolf and then, though fatally injured herself, she returns the sheep to her master, who mourns her as she dies in his arms.'

Enter Nicola Edwards, who hops about and runs around for a bit in order to represent this entire depressing chain of events.

Another thirty-two children do the same.

Behind the adjudicator sit the parents, once they have finished plastering their children with make-up and encasing them in their costumes round behind the stage. It is in this group that you would have found the high tension and dramatic sweep of emotions that I have already described. The emotional heat was simply indescribable, not least in parental attitudes to the female adjudicator.

Those whose children had been given high marks were deeply, warmly appreciative of her perceptive qualities and wise judgement. In fact, they felt that she was rather an exceptional woman. By contrast, mothers whose little girls had failed to score well were shocked and scandalised by some unknown idiot's lunatic decision to trust this blind, incompetent, spiteful, artistically barren, probably corrupt individual with the task of allotting marks to their sensitive, gifted offspring ...

Interestingly, as far as this matter of performances all being similar is concerned, my own daughter's entry in the Greek class on the Thursday was markedly distinct from *all* the others. Additionally, I was able to take a totally objective view of the adjudicator's judgement in awarding my daughter a very high mark in that same class. She was indeed an *exceptional* woman. Why things should have been so very different solely in the case of myself and my own daughter, I really could not say.

That was my immediate perception of events.

Reality hit me a little later, of course, and if you and I fail to understand the parable contained within this little account we really don't deserve to hear any more stories.

Jesus Stills a Storm

4 : 35 – 41

On that day, when evening had come, he said to them, 'Let us go across to the other side.'

And leaving the crowd behind, they took him with them in the boat, just as he was. Other boats were with him. A great wind-storm arose, and the waves beat into the boat, so that the boat was already being swamped. But he was in the stern, asleep on the cushion; and they woke him up and said to him, 'Teacher, do you not care that we are perishing?'

He woke up and rebuked the wind, and said to the sea, 'Peace! Be still!' Then the wind ceased, and there was a dead calm. He said to them, 'Why are you afraid? Have you still no faith?'

And they were filled with great awe and said to one another, 'Who then is this, that even the wind and the sea obey him?'

When you slept
On the cushion
In the boat
Did you dream the walk we took
You and I
One autumn afternoon
From that little church at Lullington
Through Littlington to Alfriston
Where ageless fields of flint and chalk
Fell seamlessly to merge and meet
With green and violet shadows
That were circling and embracing
The cathedral of the Downs?
I was in terror of a storm that day
The red and gold
Flew and fluttered round our heads

Brittle messages of loss and pain and death
The surging valley-side beyond us
Once a way to rise
I suddenly discerned
Was nothing but a dumb and loveless wall
Sad to see familiar beauty now a thing of ugliness
I dropped my gaze
You spoke a word
A firm command
Into the centre of the raging storm
And when at last I raised my eyes
I saw with grateful wonder
That the splendour had returned

Jesus Heals the Gerasene Demoniac

5 : 1 – 20

They came to the other side of the sea, to the country of the Gerasenes. And when he had stepped out of the boat, immediately a man out of the tombs with an unclean spirit met him. He lived among the tombs; and no one could restrain him any more, even with a chain; for he had often been restrained with shackles and chains, but the chains he wrenched apart, and the shackles he broke in pieces; and no one had the strength to subdue him. Night and day among the tombs and on the mountains he was always howling and bruising himself with stones.

When he saw Jesus from a distance, he ran and bowed down before him; and he shouted at the top of his voice, 'What have you to do with me, Jesus, Son of the Most High God? I adjure you by God, do not torment me.'

For he had said to him, 'Come out of the man, you unclean spirit!'

Then Jesus asked him, 'What is your name?'

He replied, 'My name is Legion; for we are many.'

He begged him earnestly not to send them out of the country. Now there on the hillside a great herd of swine was feeding; and the unclean spirits begged him, 'Send us into the swine; let us enter them.'

So he gave them permission. And the unclean spirits came out and entered the swine; and the herd, numbering about two thousand, rushed down the steep bank into the sea, and were drowned in the sea. The swineherds ran off and told it in the city and in the country. Then people came to see what it was that had happened. They came to Jesus and saw the demoniac sitting there, clothed and in his right mind, the very man who had had the legion; and they were afraid. Those who had seen what had happened to the demoniac and to the swine reported it. Then they began to beg Jesus to leave their neighbourhood. As he was getting into the boat, the man who had been possessed by demons begged him that he might be with him.

But Jesus refused, and said to him, 'Go home to your friends, and tell them how much the Lord has done for you, and what mercy he has shown you.'

And he went away and began to proclaim in the Decapolis how much Jesus had done for him; and everyone was amazed.

WHAT A SIGHT THAT MUST HAVE BEEN. AN AVALANCHE OF pork, two thousand pigs squealing and barking their way down the steep hillside, obviously no keener to be inhabited by demons than anyone else. And where did the unclean spirits go after the pigs were drowned, I wonder? Did they perish with the pigs, or did they find new human hosts to occupy? Who knows?

What I do know is that I feel a lot of sympathy with this fellow who wanted to be allowed to leave with Jesus after his healing. Apart from anything else he was well aware that, if he stayed, he would be in a minority of one. Everyone else just wanted rid of this alarming teacher who had stepped out of a boat and performed a miracle. For them, finding the man with the unclean spirit sitting quietly, dressed properly and speaking normally must have been like discovering that one whole section of landscape had changed its shape. Presumably his raving and shouting and superhuman strength had, in a way, become part of the scenery. There was something disturbingly off-centre about such a dramatic alteration in the way things were.

We might have reasonably assumed also, judging by the many comments made by Jesus about potential disciples leaving everything behind in order to follow him, that he would have encouraged the man to join his itinerant party. Instead, the master gave his latest convert an instruction that embodies a most important principle.

Sometimes we follow most effectively by staying where we are.

The most useful job this man could do was to stay where his testimony would be especially meaningful, in an area where he could share with those who had known him at his worst the story of that amazing day when a man called Jesus arrived from across the water and brought him back to stability after years of mental torment.

Perhaps in this age in particular, there tends to be a drive in those who have experienced the touch of Jesus to abandon their job or environment or normal leisure activities in order to do some kind of fulltime work for God. It feels, perhaps, like a more pure form of following. In fact, of course, there can be nothing more relentlessly fulltime than staying with and among the people who know us well, allowing them to see for themselves how being with Jesus has changed us – or not! In the seventh chapter of the first letter to the Corinthians Paul says this:

Each one should remain in the situation which he was in when God called him.

I am sure Paul did not mean this to be regarded as a shackling regulation, nor am I suggesting that the Archbishop of

Canterbury has missed his true vocation and should really be running an ironmonger's shop in Milton Keynes. As we have already seen, the disciples were called to physically follow Jesus, and some of us will certainly be called out of our former lives. It is true, though, as I and some of my fellow church members discovered during a recent course on personal evangelism, that we can become so involved in specifically Christian activities that we never meet anyone to evangelise to.

That can't be right, can it?

Can it?

A Girl Restored to Life and a Woman Healed

5 : 21 – 43

When Jesus had crossed again in the boat to the other side, a great crowd gathered around him; and he was by the sea.

Then one of the leaders of the synagogue named Jairus came and, when he saw him, fell at his feet and begged him repeatedly, 'My little daughter is at the point of death. Come and lay your hands on her, so that she may be made well, and live.'

So he went with him.

And a large crowd followed him and pressed in on him.

Now there was a woman who had been suffering from haemorrhages for twelve years. She had endured much under many physicians, and had spent all that she had; and she was no better, but rather grew worse. She had heard about Jesus, and came up behind him in the crowd and touched his cloak, for she said, 'If I but touch his clothes, I will be made well.' Immediately her haemorrhage stopped; and she felt in her body that she was healed of her disease.

Immediately aware that power had gone forth from him, Jesus turned about in the crowd and said, 'Who touched my clothes?'

And his disciples said to him, 'You see the crowd pressing in on you; how can you say, "Who touched me?"'

He looked all around to see who had done it. But the woman, knowing what had happened to her, came in fear and trembling, fell down before him, and told him the whole truth.

He said to her, 'Daughter, your faith has made you well; go in peace, and be healed of your disease.'

While he was still speaking, some people came from the leader's house to say, 'Your daughter is dead. Why trouble the teacher any further?' But overhearing what they said, Jesus said to the leader of the synagogue, 'Do not fear, only believe.' He allowed no one to follow him except Peter, James, and John, the brother of James.

When they came to the house of the leader of the synagogue, he saw a commotion, people weeping and wailing loudly. When he had entered, he said to them, 'Why do you make a commotion and weep? The child is not dead but sleeping.' And they laughed at him.

Then he put them all outside, and took the child's father and mother and those who were with him, and went in where the child was. He took her by the hand and said to her, 'Talitha cum,' which means, 'Little girl, get up!' And immediately the girl got up and began to walk about (she was twelve years of age). At this they were overcome with amazement. He strictly ordered them that no one should know this, and told them to give her something to eat.

I AM STRUCK, AS I ONCE MORE READ THIS FASCINATING account, by the high drama, and, particularly, the spontaneity of events on this one day. It makes me realise afresh how unlikely it is that Jesus spent time each morning making a list of specifically detailed plans for the coming day. I suppose if he had done, it might have looked a bit like this:

TASKS FOR TODAY

Start list – done
Pray a bit

Wake disciples
Have breakfast
Look at sea
Feel compassion
Preach a bit to crowd
Do some healings
Get cross with scribes etc.
Work on new parable(s)
Have fish lunch
Wake disciples
Set off to heal Jairus' daughter
Be touched by woman with haemorrhage on way
Discover identity of ditto
Heal ditto
Set off again
Heal Jairus' daughter
Have supper
Wake disciples ...

It seems perfectly clear to me that whilst Jesus planned his life in the broad sense, in such areas, for instance, as his tour of the smaller towns and his eventual progress towards Jerusalem, he had as little detailed idea of what each day might bring as anyone else. Do we imagine, for instance, that he *role-played* his anxiety to find out who had touched him in that surging crowd? Are we seriously suggesting that he had actually known what was going to happen and who was going to do it, but pretended he didn't just to make some kind of point? Could he really have been happy to have poor old Jairus hopping impatiently from leg to leg while he did a bit of strategic pretending? Of course not. For reasons that are none of our business, he was not given that exact piece of information at that exact moment. And what a dangerous, exhilarating, frightening, exciting way to live, don't you think? Anything could happen – anything at all. And that is, potentially anyway, still true for us. I have experienced the roller-coaster ride that God takes us on –

not very often, not as often as I would like, but enough to know that abandonment to the will of the Father beats the best of theme park rides by a very wide margin.

29

The Rejection of Jesus at Nazareth

6 : 1 – 6

He left that place and came to his hometown, and his disciples followed him. On the Sabbath he began to teach in the synagogue, and many who heard him were astounded.

They said, 'Where did this man get all this? What is this wisdom that has been given to him? What deeds of power are being done by his hands! Is not this the carpenter, the son of Mary and brother of James and Josses and Judas and Simon, and are not his sisters here with us?'

And they took offence at him.

Then Jesus said to them, 'Prophets are not without honour, except in their hometown, and among their own kin, and in their own house.' And he could do no deed of power there, except that he laid his hands on a few sick people and cured them. And he was amazed at their unbelief.

METAPHORICAL PENDULUMS ARE STRANGE, DANGEROUS, necessary things.

All right, I'm only trying to be clever, but you know what I mean. Over time, opinions or attitudes in a particular area can swing so far to avoid one pole of excess, that they move to a distant and opposite one without anyone quite realising what has happened.

The question of whose faith is required for healing is a good example. Over the past couple of decades there has been a strong reaction from many, myself included, against the idea that when sick people are not healed by prayer it is because they do not have enough faith. The strength of this reaction is not difficult to understand. Too many sufferers have had their pain increased by the thoughtlessness and insensitivity of men and women who are obsessed with the gift, and disastrously out of touch with the giver. I don't think there is as much healing happening in the church as optimists would have us suppose, but I do know that when God does heal it happens according to his own rules and not ours. People with little or no faith have been healed. People with abundant faith have been healed. There is no specific attitude or frame of mind or place or time or environment or atmosphere that will automatically guarantee or preclude healing.

Against the background of that undeniable truth I place the fact that, for some years now, I have been choosing to skate over the frequent occasions in scripture when Jesus has stated with great clarity that it is the faith of the sufferer that has enabled him or her to be made whole. In this rather sad passage, we find Jesus apparently unable to do much in the way of healing because the faith level was so low. 'Local Boy Makes Good' certainly did not apply here.

God forbid (literally) that we should return to a situation where we condemn people because they have spoiled our game by stubbornly refusing to be healed after we have repeated some pet Christian mantra over them. God is in charge of healing and he will do or not do whatever he wishes. On the other hand let us be careful not to throw the spiritual baby out with the bathwater, as we so often do (pendulums, bathwater – any old stray metaphor will do for me), by claiming that the faith of the sufferer is irrelevant to his or her prospects of healing.

Miracles grow in a bed of faith. Let us encourage each other and build each other's faith up, so that Jesus will be able to do deeds of power among us.

30

The Mission of the Twelve

6 : 7 – 13

Then he went about among the villages teaching. He called the twelve and began to send them out two by two, and gave them authority over the unclean spirits. He ordered them to take nothing for their journey except a staff; no bread, no bag, no money in their belts; but to wear sandals and not to put on two tunics.

He said to them, 'Wherever you enter a house, stay there until you leave the place. If any place will not welcome you and they refuse to hear you, as you leave, shake off the dust that is on your feet as a testimony against them.'

So they went out and proclaimed that all should repent. They cast out many demons, and anointed with oil many who were sick and cured them.

HOLD ON A MINUTE, I THOUGHT CHRISTIANS WERE SUPPOSED to be *nice* to people! What's all this about shaking the dust off your feet as a testimony against those who won't welcome you and refuse to hear you? That wouldn't go down very well in places like Bromley or Cheltenham, would it? It sounds a bit – well, a bit *rude*. I suppose it just shows how much our thinking about outreach and evangelism has changed since Jesus issued these instructions to his disciples all those years ago. We live in a very different society, and of course we must do our best to ensure that the things we say and do are relevant to the people we are trying to contact, but perhaps there is a necessary edge to effective evangelism that has got lost in this age.

I wondered about this a year or so ago when I was involved in a television studio discussion about the image of the church.

For some time we talked about how the church has to make itself attractive to young people, and we discussed the need to devise services that are lively and relevant to modern families and marginalized single folk and single parents and Ethiopian dolphins and stage-struck catamarans and sesquipedalian head-hunters and – well, just about everybody and everything really. We all agreed that we'd got to make them want to come.

Suddenly my spirit revolted. Something was wrong here. What were we saying? Here we were, talking about the desperately urgent need for men and women to repent and take advantage of the gift that a loving God is offering us in Jesus. But we were talking about it as though we were planning stalls at a fête, and hoping to attract people who were unlikely to be gracious enough to spend a few pence for the cause unless we managed to get things tarted up to a sufficiently high level. What had happened to Jesus' teaching on the *cost* of following him? Why were we not more visibly proud, in an entirely legitimate sense, of the person whom we follow? What had happened to the guts of the gospel? Where was our cosmic sense of eternity and heaven and hell?

Be relevant and plan carefully by all means. Take heed of Peter's injunction to show gentleness and respect to those who ask the reason for the hope that we have. But let us also remember that there *is* an edge to the gospel, and that we need to rediscover it.

31

The Death of
John the Baptist

6 : 14 – 29

King Herod heard of it, for Jesus' name had become known. Some were saying, 'John the baptizer has been raised from the dead; and for this reason these powers are at work in him.' But others said, 'It is Elijah.' And others said, 'It is a prophet, like one of the prophets of old.'

But when Herod heard of it, he said, 'John, whom I beheaded, has been raised.'

For Herod himself had sent men who arrested John, bound him, and put him in prison on account of Herodias, his brother Philip's wife, because Herod had married her. For John had been telling Herod, 'It is not lawful for you to have your brother's wife.' And Herodias had a grudge against him, and wanted to kill him. But she could not, for Herod feared John, knowing that he was a righteous and holy man, and he protected him. When he heard him, he was greatly perplexed; and yet he liked to listen to him.

But an opportunity came when Herod on his birthday gave a banquet for his courtiers and officers and for the leaders of Galilee. When his daughter Herodias came in and danced, she pleased Herod and his guests; and the king said to the girl, 'Ask me for whatever you wish, and I will give it.' And he solemnly swore to her, 'Whatever you ask me, I will give you, even half of my kingdom.'

She went out and said to her mother, 'What should I ask for?'

She replied, 'The head of John the baptizer.'

Immediately she rushed back to the king and requested, 'I want you to give me at once the head of John the Baptist on a platter.'

The king was deeply grieved; yet out of regard for his oaths and for the guests, he did not want to refuse her. Immediately the king sent a soldier of the guard with orders to bring John's head. He went and beheaded him in the prison, brought his head on a platter, and gave it to the girl. Then the girl gave it to her mother. When his disciples heard about it, they came and took his body, and laid it in a tomb.

W HAT NIGHTMARES HEROD MUST HAVE ENDURED. THIS pathetically grandiose gesture of his had resulted in the death of a man who, for reasons inexplicable to him, was in possession of something that not even the king's great wealth could buy. Herod had long ago boarded the non-stop express of money and power, a lavishly equipped train that would thunder through every available station and not come to a halt until it plunged into the pits of outer darkness.

And what an opportunity he wasted. Imagine having John the Baptist in your house, locked in a room downstairs, accessible exclusively to you. All that wisdom and energy and spiritual insight available, as the scheming Herodias was all too well aware, on a plate. And he blew it. Herod blew it because he was unable and unwilling to retreat from the ridiculous promise that he had made in front of his posh guests. No wonder Jesus commented on how difficult it is for a rich man to enter the Kingdom of Heaven. For Herod to have become a baptised believer would have involved slamming on the brakes of that sumptuous train and setting off again on foot, or possibly on a ramshackle little cart pulled by a donkey.

Oh, yes, if Herod really did believe that Jesus was John returned from the dead and likely to 'come and get him' at any moment, his nights must have been hell.

And, let's face it, this happens on all sorts of different levels. Bridget and I are not rich in the context of average lifestyles in the west, but compared with most of the rest of the world we are wealthy beyond belief. There was one moment, famous in the annals of the Plass family, when this realisation hit us forcibly. We were having our Victorian farmhouse kitchen modernised. It needed it. For instance, the floor was made of brick tiles set in mud. Whenever it rained really hard worms came up through the cracks between the bricks, had a look round to get their bearings, then burrowed back down in bewilderment. I kid you not! That was just one problem whose solution was way overdue. There were many more. The work began.

One phase of this building work involved the knocking down of two old pantry walls so that the usable length of the kitchen would be increased. This worked very well except that the stable door from the back-yard still opened inwards, occupying the space that had been saved by demolishing the pantry. There was only one solution. We asked the builders to take the door down, brick up the old doorway, and put a new door in where the pantry wall had been. It was while they were in the middle of this operation that I happened to be watching television when news came of some appalling natural disaster on the other side of the world. Three million people were facing starvation. I thought about what was happening in our kitchen.

'Do you realise,' I said to Bridget, who happened to walk in at that moment, 'what they're probably saying in heaven?'

'What are they probably saying in heaven?'

'They're probably saying, "Three million people are starving, and the Plasses are having their door moved three feet to the left." '

We mustn't be silly about these things. If I were to sell absolutely everything that I have and give it to the poor I would immediately become dependent on someone else's money. On the other hand, I would do well to remember Herod's nightmares, and make sure I am able and willing to stop this train and get off, if that is what is required of me.

32

Feeding the Five Thousand

6 : 30 – 44

The apostles gathered around Jesus, and told him all that they had done and taught.

He said to them, 'Come away to a deserted place all by yourselves and rest a while.' For many were coming and going, and they had no leisure even to eat. And they went away in the boat to a deserted place by themselves.

Now many saw them going and recognized them, and they hurried there on foot from all the towns and arrived ahead of them. As he went ashore, he saw a great crowd; and he had compassion for them, because they were like sheep without a shepherd; and he began to teach them many things.

When it grew late, his disciples came to him and said, 'This is a deserted place, and the hour is now very late; send them away so that they may go into the surrounding country and villages and buy something for themselves to eat.'

But he answered them, 'You give them something to eat.'

They said to him, 'Are we to go and buy two hundred denarii worth of bread, and give it to them to eat?'

And he said to them, 'How many loaves have you? Go and see.'

When they had found out, they said, 'Five, and two fish.' Then he ordered them to get all the people to sit down in groups on the green grass.

So they sat down in groups of hundreds and of fifties. Taking the five loaves and the two fish, he looked up to heaven, and blessed and broke the loaves, and gave them to his disciples to set before the people; and he divided the two fish among them all. And all ate and were filled; and they took up twelve baskets full of broken pieces and of the fish. Those who had eaten the loaves numbered five thousand men.

I KNOW THAT SOME CHRISTIAN PARENTS DISCOURAGE THEIR children from a belief in Father Christmas. Christians should deal only with the truth, they point out, and in any case, what could be more ludicrous than the idea of a fat man dressed in red who is able to visit every home in the world on the same night, leaving presents for the children of the house?

Well, of course, much more ludicrous than that is the idea of a man who is really God coming down to live with us on this planet and doing all sorts of incredible things that have no natural explanation. Here is one of those incredible things happening in this passage. Five thousand people need to be fed, and, for once, it is like some fantastic child's story happening in real life. A few loaves and a couple of fish are miraculously turned into enough food to feed every single person and leave twelve whole baskets of scraps that were not needed. By the way, it's worth taking some time to really think through the significance of those extra baskets. As we shall see in a moment, the disciples didn't, and probably wished they had.

Do you find it exciting that the power and practices of the Holy Spirit make a lot of so-called fantasy fiction seem as dull as the sanitary inspector's handbook? You know what it all means, don't you? I said it earlier, but it will certainly bear repeating. It means that *anything* is possible. Today, as you read these words, *anything* is possible. Got it? *Anything*.

Should children believe in Father Christmas? Sounds to me like pretty good practise for the real thing.

33

Jesus Walks on the Water

6 : 45 – 52

Immediately he made his disciples get into the boat and go on ahead to the other side, to Bethsaida, while he dismissed the crowd. After saying farewell to them, he went up on the mountain to pray.

When evening came, the boat was out on the sea, and he was alone on the land. When he saw that they were straining at the oars against an adverse wind, he came towards them early in the morning, walking on the sea. He intended to pass them by. But when they saw him walking on the sea, they thought it was a ghost and cried out; for they all saw him and were terrified.

But immediately he spoke to them and said, 'Take heart, it is I; do not be afraid.'

Then he got into the boat with them and the wind ceased. And they were utterly astounded, for they did not understand about the loaves, but their hearts were hardened.

WHY DID JESUS INTEND TO PASS THEM BY? WHY DID HE not simply head for the boat, climb over the side and sort everything out? After all, that's what happened in the end anyway. My own theory, vulnerable as ever to broadsides from the experts, is that after all that preaching and all that food distribution he just wanted a little time to himself. He had already sent the disciples on ahead, so, in theory, they were accounted for. After the crowd had dispersed it must have been such a joy to climb up onto the mountain and find refreshment through contact with his Father. Later, a gentle stroll down to the seashore before setting off towards the place where he would meet the disciples in the morning.

Those among my readers who have parented or been responsible for teenage children will be all too familiar with what happens next. You think you've got everything sorted out so that you can leave them to get on with it, whatever *it* is. You've provided the means to do it and you've made the arrangements for meeting later. As far as you know, every eventuality is covered. Now, surely, you have earned yourself a little time on your own. What could possibly go wrong? The phone rings …

In this case it was not a phone ringing. It was the sight of those hapless disciples struggling to make way against the force of an adverse wind and not making a very good job of it.

Presumably Jesus was hoping that the mere sight of him passing by would be reassuring enough to give them new resolve in their battle with the elements. That would leave him free to be alone for a little longer. If that was what he thought, he was wrong. Far from being reassured they were terrified by the sight of something that was too far outside their experience to be easily accommodated.

Notice that Jesus changed his mind. He had intended to pass them by, but seeing how afraid they were, he changed his mind and got into the boat with them. Are you comfortable with the idea that the Son of God might change his mind? I am. A man who never knew what it was to change his mind would not be truly man.

We know, from the master's reaction to his disciples' lack of faith on other occasions, that Jesus would have been amazed and baffled by their fear. These twelve men had just witnessed the feeding of five thousand people with five small loaves and two small fish. This mind-blowing event had followed hard on the heels of their own experience in ministry of seeing people healed and delivered from demons. How, Jesus must have wondered, could they still be so lacking in trust, that storms and 'ghosts' were able to fill them with such terror? Twelve baskets of food had been collected after yesterday's meal. Could they not understand the message of that excess food? In the Kingdom of Heaven the provision of material benefits, including such things as physical safety, is a piece of cake, or bread, or fish.

But what am I talking about? I am no better than those disciples. After more than thirty years of being looked after by God I still experience a lot of fear. Please pray for me.

34

Healing the Sick
in Gennesaret

6 : 53 – 56

When they had crossed over, they came to land at Gennesaret and moored the boat. When they got out of the boat, people at once recognized him, and rushed about that whole region and began to bring the sick on mats to wherever they heard he was. And wherever he went, into villages or cities or farms, they laid the sick in the marketplaces, and begged him that they might touch even the fringe of his cloak; and all who touched it were healed.

T HEY WERE *RUSHING* AROUND!

This all sounds very wonderful, doesn't it? And for those who were healed and their friends and families it undoubtedly was. But read this passage again. Even my limited experience of being involved in a travelling ministry allows me to tell you with confidence that it must have been something of a nightmare as well. There were no Forte Crest Hotels for speakers to disappear into in those days, and, unlike many of us modern, so-called Christian speakers, Jesus was never afraid to put his

91

money where his mouth had been, as it were. Wherever he turned, wherever he stayed, whatever he did, eating, drinking, sleeping or waking, there they were by their tens and by their hundreds. Men and women with desperate longing in their eyes and a tremulous hope in their hearts. And who could blame them for coming? Not me. Certainly not him. A unique opportunity. The man who was famous for being able to make people better – really, really better – had come to their village or city or farm. Never mind if he was who he said he was or not. It was a chance not to be missed.

'Quick! Roll young Benjamin onto a mat and we'll take him along to the market place. This could be his only chance – hurry! Oh, and pop round quickly and tell them next door but three as well. Let's go!'

Jesus loved to see people's sins forgiven and their bodies healed. Nobody can doubt that after reading the gospels. But think back for a moment to his encounter with the woman suffering from haemorrhages. When she touched the hem of his cloak Jesus felt the power go out of him. I have no idea what that means, but I suspect that when hundreds of people did exactly the same thing in this area of Gennesaret it must have produced a draining, spiritual exhaustion that we simply cannot imagine. Add to that the more familiar natural exhaustion caused by the need to give each person very special and particular attention (the Son of God never doled out ministry like food parcels), and you will begin to see how very, very weary Jesus must have become.

And always, buzzing around at the edge of the crowd like a swarm of gnats, were the scribes and the Pharisees, narrowly watching his every move, waiting for him to put a foot wrong, hoping and waiting for an excuse to have another go.

35

The Tradition
of the Elders

7 : 1 – 23

Now when the Pharisees and some of the scribes who had come
from Jerusalem gathered around him, they noticed that some of his
disciples were eating with defiled hands, that is, without washing
them. (For the Pharisees, and all the Jews, do not eat unless they
thoroughly wash their hands, thus observing the tradition of the
elders; and they do not eat anything from the market unless they
wash it; and there are also many other traditions that they observe,
the washing of cups, pots, and bronze kettles.)

So the Pharisees and the scribes asked him, 'Why do your
disciples not live according to the tradition of the elders, but eat
with defiled hands?'

He said to them, 'Isaiah prophesied rightly about you hypo-
crites, as it is written, "This people honours me with their lips, but
their hearts are far from me; in vain do they worship me, teaching
human precepts as doctrines." You abandon the commandment of
God and hold to human tradition.'

Then he said to them, 'You have a fine way of rejecting the
commandment of God in order to keep your tradition! For Moses
said, "Honour your father and your mother"; and, "Whoever
speaks evil of father or mother must surely die." But you say that if
anyone tells father or mother, "Whatever support you might have
had from me is Corban" (that is, an offering to God) – then you no
longer permit doing anything for a father or mother, thus making
void the word of God through your tradition that you have handed
on. And you do many things like this.'

Then he called the crowd again and said to them, 'Listen to
me, all of you, and understand: there is nothing outside a person
that by going in can defile, but the things that come out are what
defile.'

When he had left the crowd and entered the house, his disciples asked him about the parable.

He said to them, 'Then do you also fail to understand? Do you
not see that whatever goes into a person from outside cannot
defile, since it enters, not the heart but the stomach, and goes out
into the sewer?'

(Thus he declared all foods clean.)

And he said, 'It is what comes out of a person that defiles. For
it is from within, from the human heart, that evil intentions come:
fornication, theft, murder, adultery, avarice, wickedness, deceit,
licentiousness, envy, slander, pride, folly. All these evil things
come from within, and they defile a person.'

T HE ONLY THING TO DO WITH GNATS IS TO SWAT THEM, AND
that is exactly what Jesus did. The Pharisees and scribes had
turned faith in God into a ludicrously convoluted metaphor
instead of a reality, a matter of the heart. No doubt Jesus had
known and met some of the victims of the spiritual fraudulence
that allowed these twisters to neglect their own parents, and
there is a sense of anger – of outrage – in his response to them
that could only have been met with fury or shame.

Now, some may wish to say that this issue has little application to modern life, but I would have to disagree, especially as
I have been guilty of something very similar myself. In the years
immediately following the publication of *The Sacred Diary of
Adrian Plass* invitations to speak to churches and groups of
Christians came thick and fast. I was amazed, flattered and
overwhelmed that all these people seemed to want *me*. Until
very recently I had had nothing to offer, and an entirely negative view of myself. I accepted just about every invitation with
alacrity, disappearing two, three or even four times in a week
to travel to different parts of the country. Those were exhilarating, heady days for me, but I know for a fact that, through my
continual absence, my wife and children suffered far more
neglect than they should have. I also know that I extinguished
any qualms I might have felt by telling myself that I was engaged

in the 'Lord's work'. It is very easily done, I'm afraid. If you are worried that this might apply to you, I suggest that you look into your own heart. The answer will be there. Do face it squarely. I didn't until it was almost too late.

Incidentally, this passage assists in scotching the view that Jesus, by saying, 'Who is my mother?' was in some way rejecting or dissociating himself from a special connection with her. Jesus was many things. He was not a hypocrite. You can be sure that if he was telling these characters off for neglecting their parents, he was certainly not doing the same to his own.

One other point. The writer of the gospel is at pains to point out that the comment about what goes in and what comes out of the body is a clear indication from Jesus that all foods are, in themselves, clean. When are we going to simply accept this very straightforward piece of teaching? I have heard such nonsense on the subject. We have enough genuine problems without having to cast demons out of turnips, or finding it necessary to marinade pickled onions in prayer. Honestly!

36

The Syrophoenician Woman's Faith

7 : 24 – 30

From there he set out and went away to the region of Tyre. He entered a house and did not want anyone to know he was there. Yet he could not escape notice, but a woman whose little daughter had an unclean spirit immediately heard about him, and she came and bowed down at his feet. Now the woman was a Gentile, of Syrophoenician origin. She begged him to cast the demon out of her daughter.

He said to her, 'Let the children be fed first, for it is not fair to take the children's food and throw it to the dogs.'

But she answered him, 'Sir, even the dogs under the table eat the children's crumbs.'

Then he said to her, 'For saying that, you may go – the demon has left your daughter.' So she went home, found the child lying on the bed, and the demon gone.

D O YOU RECALL THAT LITTLE SPOT OF IDLE SPECULATION we indulged in earlier? Let's do it again.

Jesus, exhausted from his work and desperately needing a break, arrives in Tyre and decides to tuck himself away for a little while in a house belonging to one of his sympathetic supporters. The nearest he was ever going to come to that Forte Crest Hotel we mentioned earlier. We know that he is not intending to do any healing or deliverance on this particular day, because he doesn't want anyone to know that he is there.

Here, incidentally, is yet another reminder that, as far as we can see, Jesus only received divine revelation on what we modern people call a need-to-know basis. As we read the gospels we learn that he was shocked, he was amazed, he wept, he was tempted, he grew angry. These are the spontaneous reactions of a man to events that presented themselves as unexpected experiences. How, in all seriousness, could it have been otherwise if his life as a vulnerable human being was to mean anything? It is theoretically the same for us in the twenty-first century. You and I may have problems about being truly open to the Spirit of God, but, as Jesus himself implied in the twelfth chapter of Luke, he will give us the words and the knowledge when we need them.

So, where were we? Ah, yes, here is Jesus leaning back against the wall in a corner with his eyes shut, enjoying the breeze running through the house but keeping well away from the windows. He thinks he will be doing no healing today, but in this he is less than omniscient. The Syrophoenician woman, her urgency and determination fuelled by a mother's love, has, so I have learned from those who know the geography of the region, travelled a very long way to find help for her beloved daughter. Suddenly she is there, kneeling at his feet, a person with a favour to ask, if ever there was one.

Was the Son of God tempted to groan and sigh and click his tongue and slap the seat beside him in annoyance? Well, perhaps, but I feel quite sure he did not succumb to that temptation. Possibly, though, he might have hoped that his first reply would send her away and allow him to stay in precisely the comfortable position that he had managed to find against a Saviour-shaped hollow in the wall.

Not a chance. In the end the combination of love, passionate need and wit was irresistible. As a man who specialised in words and witty retorts himself, Jesus must have been delighted with the answer she gave him.

I wonder, did he say, 'That's *very* good!'?

People sometimes ask me if I think Jesus laughed a lot. I doubt if his life produced much cause to guffaw wildly, but I would be prepared to bet that this woman's words brought a smile to his face, at the very least. She got exactly what she wanted.

What a marvellous, tear-streaked journey back home for this woman. The very next time she saw her daughter the child would be lying on her bed, clear-eyed and calm. Jesus had said it would be so – just after she made him smile.

Mainly idle speculation, of course ...

37

Jesus Cures a Deaf Man

7 : 31 – 37

Then he returned from the region of Tyre, and went by way of
Sidon towards the Sea of Galilee, in the region of the Decapolis.
They brought to him a deaf man who had an impediment in his
speech; and they begged him to lay his hand on him. He took him
aside in private, away from the crowd, and put his fingers into his
ears, and he spat and touched his tongue.

Then looking up to heaven, he sighed and said to him,
'Ephphatha,' that is, 'Be opened.'

And immediately his ears were opened, his tongue was
released, and he spoke plainly. Then Jesus ordered them to tell no
one; but the more he ordered them, the more zealously they proclaimed it. They were astounded beyond measure, saying, 'He has
done everything well; he even makes the deaf to hear and the
mute to speak.'

SENSITIVE AS EVER, JESUS TAKES THIS DEAF MAN WELL AWAY
from crowds and noise so that he will not be overwhelmed
by a cacophony of sounds when his hearing is restored. Are the
fingers in the ears and the spitting on the tongue part of the
healing process, or, as seems more likely, was Jesus simply mim-
ing what he was about to do? Another interesting but unanswerable question. But here is one indisputable fact. For this
man, the first sound to emerge from a lifelong well of silence
was the voice of the Son of God. Not a bad way to start, was
it? For as long as he lived he would never forget the voice that
called him out of silence and bewilderment into a new way of
life.

It may seem blunderingly symbolic to say so, but many of
the Christians that I meet have forgotten the tone and content

of the voice that first called them to follow their master without question. There are so many other voices that come crashing in with opinions and doctrines and advice and temptations and distractions.

Move away from those other sounds to a private place away from the crowd. Close your eyes. Listen hard. Do you hear that voice coming out of the silence, the voice that first commanded your eyes to be opened and your ears to be unblocked? Do your vision and your hearing need to be healed again? His gentle touch is upon you. Open your eyes and listen with your ears. There are old and new things to see and hear.

38

Feeding the Four Thousand

8 : 1 – 10

In those days when there was again a great crowd without anything to eat, he called his disciples and said to them, 'I have compassion for the crowd, because they have been with me now for three days and have nothing to eat. If I send them away hungry to their homes, they will faint on the way — and some of them have come from a great distance.'

His disciples replied, 'How can one feed these people with bread here in the desert?'

He asked them, 'How many loaves do you have?'

They said, 'Seven.'

Then he ordered the crowd to sit down on the ground; and he took the seven loaves, and after giving thanks he broke them and gave them to his disciples to distribute; and they distributed them to the crowd. They had also a few small fish; and after blessing them, he ordered that these too should be distributed. They ate and were filled; and they took up the broken pieces left over, seven baskets full. Now there were about four thousand people. And he sent them away. And immediately he got into the boat with his disciples and went to the district of Dalmanutha.

WHY HAS MARK DESCRIBED A SECOND OCCASION ON WHICH thousands of people are fed with a few loaves and fishes? A variety of theories has been propounded over the years. Some say that it is actually the same event, but repeated with slightly different details for some obscure reason. Others maintain that one group was made up of Jews and the other of Gentiles, thus making the whole thing deeply symbolic, if more than a little unconvincing.

My own earth-shattering, revolutionary theory – brace yourself! – is that there really were two occasions when roughly the same thing happened, and that Mark decided to record both of them. How about that for a radical thought! And if you want to say to me that the disciples cannot possibly have been that obtuse twice in a row, then I can only conclude that you have not read the gospels with due care and attention, and that you are not a member of any church that I would recognise. We disciples were and are capable of being as thick as several short planks.

Could that be exactly what lies behind Mark's decision to include a second example of supernatural mass-catering? With their earlier experience of huge numbers of people having a more than adequate lunch produced from the slimmest resources, it is truly amazing that the disciples came out with more or less the same objections. Mark is exhorting us to remember what God has done, at the times when we are wondering what he is going to do.

39

The Demand for a Sign

8 : 11 – 13

The Pharisees came and began to argue with him, asking him for a sign from heaven, to test him. And he sighed deeply in his spirit and said, 'Why does this generation ask for a sign? Truly I tell you, no sign will be given to this generation.' And he left them, and getting into the boat again, he went across to the other side.

MANY YEARS AGO I WROTE ABOUT A MAN WHO SAID THAT he would do the difficult and unwelcome thing that God was asking of him if a midget wearing a Japanese admiral's uniform came and knocked on his door at a particular hour of the day. This visitation, he said, would be a final sign that God really did want him to perform the task in question. You will not be greatly surprised to hear that no such weirdly dressed, vertically challenged person appeared at the specified time, so the man was able to happily persuade himself that God had changed his mind.

This sounds absurd. It is absurd. And yet, at the time when I was converted there was a general feeling that specific, inch by inch, testimony paperback-style, fully guaranteed guidance was available at any time of the day or night. Of course, this was all part of the excitement that many believers were experiencing at what seemed to be the dawn of a new age of Spirit-directed Christianity (so much better than that tired old non-Spirit-directed Christianity we all felt).

We devoured books appearing on the market at that time that chronicled the development of individual ministries. These exciting volumes were crammed with miracles of heavenly timing and healing and visions and coincidences that were not really coincidences, and flashes of guidance that illuminated the path of the protagonist like those rows of floor-lights on aeroplanes that we hope we shall never need to use. Reading those books was like reading a modern version of Acts. We wanted our lives to offer us the same kinds of adventure. All of this was understandable, and some of it was good and valuable, but there were times when our frantic desire to see the hand and hear the voice of God in everything that happened pushed us over the line from faith to superstition. Ouija-board-style Christianity is one of the devil's greatest triumphs.

Let us be clear. God gives signs to men and women. He always has done in the past, he does in this age, and I expect he always will. Sometimes these signs are dramatic, and sometimes they are not. Often they are not there when we want them and think we need them. The thing to remember is that God is rather more practical than his followers. If you or I need a sign we shall certainly get one. If we do not need a sign (and a lot of people would do better to read their Bibles or listen to their consciences and their hearts than look for shapes in the sky) then we may safely and calmly assume that God has allowed us all the information necessary for making a good decision.

Pray always, use your commonsense to make decisions, don't ask for confirmation of something you already know in your heart but don't want to face, ask God to stop you if you go wrong, read the Bible, expect signs, expect no signs, don't get deceived into thirsting for 'magic', and do enjoy the adventure. That's what we should do. I achieve bits of it sometimes. How about you?

40

The Yeast of the
Pharisees and of Herod

8 : 14 – 21

Now the disciples had forgotten to bring any bread; and they had
only one loaf with them in the boat. And he cautioned them, saying, 'Watch out – beware of the yeast of the Pharisees and the
yeast of Herod.'

They said to one another, 'It is because we have no bread.'

And becoming aware of it, Jesus said to them, 'Why are you
talking about having no bread? Do you still not perceive or understand? Are your hearts hardened? Do you have eyes, and fail to
see? Do you have ears, and fail to hear? And do you not remember? When I broke the five loaves for the five thousand, how many
baskets full of broken pieces did you collect?'

They said to him, 'Twelve.'

'And the seven for the four thousand, how many baskets full of
broken pieces did you collect?'

And they said to him, 'Seven.'

Then he said to them, 'Do you not yet understand?'

WEARYING FOR JESUS. THE MEMBERS OF THIS WATER-BORNE
class of Galilean juniors were a couple of fishing boats
short of a fleet, to say the least. How was it possible that they
could respond to the warning their master gave them by mut-
tering on about a shortage of bread? After those two extraordinary experiences of Jesus feeding the masses might it not have
occurred to them that, in the circumstances, having one loaf
available for a mere thirteen people was really quite extrava-
gant? We would never have been as obtuse as those silly old
disciples, would we? No-o-o, of course we wouldn't.

Actually, the problem Jesus was having with his disciples has not changed from that day to this. We human beings, Christians included, routinely default to a setting that is primarily dedicated to our material welfare, and genuinely changing priorities is much more difficult than writing with the wrong hand, and almost as difficult as riding one of those bicycles that go left when you steer right and right when you steer left.

What it all boils down to is that, in deciding to follow Jesus, we are giving up the right to make any decision about our own lives that moves outside the will of God. That hurts. No wonder Jesus said that we must carefully count the cost of following him.

On the day before writing this I travelled back home from the North by train. This involved a number of changes, and I have never known such a succession of delays and problems in my life. Every now and then a voice would announce cheerily over the loudspeaker system that a train crew had failed to turn up, or that a train experiencing mechanical difficulties was limping towards the station, preventing the trains behind it from travelling at normal speed, or that there was a fault in the track that must be rectified before trains could proceed. I became more and more annoyed as time went by. After the third delay was announced I flopped down onto a bench on the platform of the station where I was stranded and prepared myself for half an hour of grumpiness and sulking. Five minutes into my misery a thought struck me. This was not my time. This was God's time. This thirty minutes of apparent non-activity was part of an over-all plan, or an opportunity for something else to happen, depending on which way you looked at it. I did not have the right to immerse myself in negative feelings, because wherever I am and whatever is happening there is work to be done. These reflections transfigured that hour. I didn't do so well during the next delay, but there you are ...

It applies to everything, I'm afraid.

I know that a friend badly needs a visit, but it's wet outside and the fire and the television beckon. I could go some other time. Why shouldn't I settle down and enjoy myself?

Someone has let me down badly. Surely it's my right to indulge the hostility and hurt that their actions have caused. Why should I even think about forgiving them?

My wife announces that she would like me to do some digging in her beloved garden. But I've already worked hard all morning. I was looking forward to doing something that *I* wanted to do. Why should I do something just because it will make *her* happy?

The answer to all these questions is, of course, that I can do exactly what I want. I am perfectly free to do as I wish, just as Jesus was.

41

Jesus Cures
a Blind Man
at Bethsaida

8 : 22 – 26

They came to Bethsaida. Some people brought a blind man to him and begged him to touch him. He took the blind man by the hand and led him out of the village; and when he had put saliva on his eyes and laid his hands on him, he asked him, 'Can you see anything?'

And the man looked up and said, 'I can see people, but they look like trees, walking.'

Then Jesus laid his hands on his eyes again; and he looked intently and his sight was restored, and he saw everything clearly. Then he sent him away to his home, saying, 'Do not even go into the village.'

D O YOU THINK THIS MAN MIGHT HAVE BEEN A LITTLE disappointed when he looked up and saw fuzzy shapes moving about like man-sized trees instead of having his vision fully restored? Not enough saliva? Hands not laid on for quite long enough? Surely the reason for his incomplete healing could not be that banal. Or was it simply that Jesus was aware of the potentially negative effects of sudden, total restoration of sight? An abrupt flood of light and images after total darkness would have been an uncomfortable shock, to say the least.

I suspect that there is a sense in which all of us are being taken through a gradual process of attaining full spiritual sight. I get very impatient sometimes. I yearn for God to reveal himself to me in new and more dynamic ways. I try to tell myself that my motivation is pure.

'Don't you see, God,' I protest, 'that if you furnish me with one or two really startling revelations it will give a terrific boost to my ministry? It's you I'm thinking of …'

It's actually me I'm thinking of usually. Sometimes, for instance, when I trip over a doubt, it feels as if a good juicy revelation would haul me to my feet and get me moving again. In my more sensible moments I know perfectly well that, as long as I am genuinely trying to be open to the working of the Holy Spirit in my life, I will always be seeing exactly what I need to see, no more and no less. God does not want me to be stumbling in the darkness, nor does he want me blinded by a light that is too great for me to bear at the moment. And the extent to which another man or woman can or cannot see is quite irrelevant. We are precious in his sight, and so, increasingly and at precisely the right speed, is he in ours.

Peter's Declaration about Jesus

8 : 27 – 30

Jesus went on with his disciples to the villages of Caesarea Philippi; and on the way he asked his disciples, 'Who do people say that I am?'

And they answered him, 'John the Baptist; and others, Elijah; and still others, one of the prophets.'

He asked them, 'But who do you say that I am?'

Peter answered him, 'You are the Messiah.' And he sternly ordered them not to tell anyone about him.

WHEN I READ ABOUT THIS KEY MOMENT IN THE MINISTRY of Jesus, so briefly recorded here, my imagination goes haywire. If we had been there, and if we had had the eyes to see, might we have looked up and seen the numberless hosts of paradise and God himself leaning forward on the edge of their heavenly seats, waiting with bated breath and in a profound, cosmic silence for Peter to answer his master's question? Such a crucial question, because Peter's grasp of the answer would be, not so much like a pebble falling in a pond, as like a gigantic asteroid landing in a mighty ocean. From that one man and a handful of others like him, tidal waves of faith would sweep across the world, changing it forever.

I don't know exactly how the heavenly hosts would have reacted to those four sweet words of Peter's, but I presume it must have been the divine version of upper cutting the air with their fists, and shouting 'Yes!!'

Jesus may have been stern when he told them to keep quiet about it, but nobody could convince me that he was anything but thrilled when he realised that those closest to him had got the main message. I know that good feeling. Those who love us know who we really are, in our case the not-so-good things as well as the better part of us. That doesn't matter. We all need to be known by someone. It is like putting your heart in a safe place.

By the way, that important question that Peter answered is one that Jesus will ask each one of us at some point in our walk with him.

'Never mind what people in or out of church think,' he will say. 'Never mind what famous Christians and ministers and theologians and writers who think they're funny and your best mate and the members of your house-group and the bloke at work and Victorian hymn-writers think. Who do *you* say that I am?'

Well?

43

Jesus Foretells His Death and Resurrection

8 : 31 – 33

Then he began to teach them that the Son of Man must undergo great suffering, and be rejected by the elders, the chief priests, and the scribes, and be killed, and after three days rise again. He said all this quite openly. And Peter took him aside and began to rebuke him. But turning and looking at his disciples, he rebuked Peter and said, 'Get behind me, Satan! For you are setting your mind not on divine things but on human things.'

REACTIONS TO THIS ACCOUNT OF THE STARTLING MOMENT when Jesus turned to the rock on which he intended to build his church, and addressed him as 'Satan', tend to focus on Peter, and how such a blast of a rebuke must have made him feel. The poor bloke was only doing his best, after all, wasn't he? That's what I've always felt. It seems a bit much. Out of perfectly charitable motives you take a friend aside and encourage him to cut out all that silly talk about dying, and in front of everyone he accuses you of being the embodiment of evil. A bit over the top, perhaps? How would your average, polite, modern Christian have responded to Peter's admonition?

'Thanks ever so much, old chap, for taking such an interest. I know exactly where you're coming from and I do appreciate and value what you're saying. It's just that I do feel there is a pretty good reason for going ahead with things, and I hope you won't be too offended if I don't take your very well-meant advice. So, thanks again, and I do hope this won't affect our friendship ...'

The aspect I have never really focussed on before is that this incident is, in fact, more about Jesus than it is about Peter. Back in chapter three, after the passage in which Jesus is accused of being in league with Beelzubel, we were thinking about the choice between obedience and human response that must have confronted Jesus over and over again, simply because he was an authentic man and therefore tempted as we are. Here, in a frozen moment of history, is a vivid example of the new Adam summoning all his resolve in order to make one of these tough choices.

How very tempting it must have been for this man who had to keep on remembering that he was also God. It never really occurred to me until now that the vehemence of that rebuke may have reflected, not so much the depth and intensity of Peter's evil intentions, as the powerful inclination in Jesus himself to collude with the notion that he might evade or avoid the suffering and death that was clearly essential to the success of his mission.

'Do you honestly think,' he might have gone on to say to Peter, 'that I *want* to be rejected and killed and all the rest of it? Almost everything in me would love to say to you, "Yes, yes, of course you're right. There's no need for me to get carried away. Why don't we get the rest of the lads over here and ask them what they think?" And if I were to do that, Peter, they'd all say exactly the same as you, wouldn't they? And that would make it even more difficult for me to stick to what I know is right. So just *don't* tempt me, *please*!'

And I am sure we all know that feeling, if only in a small way, don't we? I certainly do. I am talking about that warm, fuzzy feeling you get when some nice, well meaning person points out all the very good, very sound reasons why you should abandon the path of tough obedience that is clearly beckoning and do the safer, easier thing. The reassuring arguments of a good friend are very seductive, but when they endanger the work of the Holy Spirit they must be resisted as if they issued from the devil himself.

44

Followers must take up their cross

8 : 34

He called the crowd with his disciples, and said to them, 'If any want to become my followers, let them deny themselves and take up their cross and follow me.'

ONE VITAL AND AGONISING ASPECT OF PETER'S INDIVIDUAL cross was his gradual realisation that he was not to be allowed to take initiatives that, from the worldly and objective point of view, promised to produce the most appropriate and loving courses of action. The disciples found it extremely difficult to predict the response of their master to any given situation, simply because he only ever did what he saw his Father doing. Peter needed to learn, as many of us modern Christians need to learn, how the creative ingenuity of God demands the *right* reaction, as opposed to the logical or traditional one. Read the tenth chapter of Acts, and you will see that Peter was still learning that lesson, even after the Holy Spirit had come.

Our individual crosses come in many shapes and sizes. Some of us are called upon to suffer the most appalling hardship and pain for the sake of the gospel. Many more of us wrestle with the ordinary but by no means trivial burdens that accompany our attempts to follow Jesus faithfully from day to day. It takes years (well, it's taken me years anyway) to understand the importance of the individual role that God has given us in our own immediate environment.

Take my friend Sydney. He's a very good example of the wide variety of shapes that crosses come in. One of his crosses is very strange. It is shaped like a cat.

The true and tragic tale of Sydney and the cat next door is a tale whose implications would have seriously tested the faith of a Daniel. If it had happened to Abraham, he might have never have left home, and I would not be writing these words today.

Sydney, unmarried and in his early fifties, was employed by our local parish church as a pastoral worker. As well as visiting the elderly and the sick, he assisted in church services throughout the week and preached from time to time. Mild, kindly and benign in manner and appearance, Sydney was a frequent sight around our town as he dutifully pedalled his beloved bicycle from one area of need to another.

The cat in the tale lived in the house next to Sydney's. According to Sydney he was a bulky, insolently staring creature of a muddy, indeterminate colour. Not an attractive animal. His elderly mistress, Mrs Potter, was not a church-attender, nor was she an easy person to befriend. Despite working extremely hard over the years, at the time when these events occurred Sydney had only managed to achieve a nodding acquaintance with his neighbour.

Sydney hated cats. For all I know it was his only vice, but he was not a willing slave to his one weakness. For a long time he was just about able to tolerate Mrs Potter's cat using his garden occasionally as a short-cut to somewhere else. It was when the animal selected a particularly cherished flower-bed as his regular and preferred toilet area that something in Sydney finally snapped. Picking up an old shoe one day, he flung it through the window with as much power as he could muster, catching the startled cat in mid-toilet and sending it scuttling back over the fence to its own territory.

Sydney's unaccustomed surge of satisfaction and triumph was short-lived. Mrs Potter appeared at his door within minutes to lodge a furious complaint. She had witnessed the whole appalling episode from an upstairs window, she stated, and was profoundly shocked that a man who publicly professed to occupy a representative role in the Church of England could have behaved in such a cruel and violent manner towards a dumb beast who was doing him no harm.

Sydney was mortified. He grovelled and repented, but to no avail. Even the hard-won nodding acquaintanceship appeared to be at an end. He, a Christian, had failed to love his neighbour as himself. Instead, in a moment of madness he had slung a shoe at her cat.

Sydney sat guiltily at home on the evening following the outrage, wondering what he could possibly do to make amends. Suddenly an idea struck him. In a corner of the garage next to his house stood a bag containing a little coal left over from the time before his central heating had been fitted. Mrs Potter was a widow living on a state pension, and she still used a large open fire in her sitting room when she could afford it. He would give her the coal as a peace offering. Yes, that might do the trick.

On the following day he knocked on his neighbour's front

door, offered another stream of humble and profuse apologies, and presented the bag of coal with his best wishes. Patently unimpressed by the apologies, Mrs Potter's eyes did light up at the sight of fuel for her fire, and Sydney returned to his own house happy in the knowledge that, at the very least, a thaw seemed to have set in in their frozen relationship.

His optimism was sadly misplaced. Some hours later, on that fateful chilly autumn evening, Mrs Potter emptied the bag of coal on to her fire, then settled back in cosy anticipation of the blaze that would result.

Psychiatrists tell us that some failure of memory is subconsciously deliberate. That may or may not be true. It is certainly true that Sidney had forgotten that, in addition to the coal, there had been some small pieces of broken glass in the bottom of that bag that had stood for so long in the corner of his garage. Having attained a certain heat in the depths of the fire these small pieces exploded, shooting out into the sitting-room and severely injuring Mrs Potter's cat.

Sydney felt obliged to pay the vast and ongoing veterinary bills that arose from this incident. Furthermore, he ruefully reported that the likelihood of Mrs Potter applying for membership of a church capable of employing a psychopath who, in her view, had embarked on a coldly cynical campaign to murder her cat, was less even than in past years.

Where was God in all this? It is very hard to tell. But what wouldn't we all give to be a fly on the wall when Sydney meets Job in heaven and the two of them have a chance to compare notes?

'With me it was boils,' says Job.

'With me,' says Sydney sadly, 'it was a cat.'

We may laugh, but the fact is that Job and Sydney and you and I (and Peter, two thousand years ago) are asked by God to carry the burden that has been placed before us, however small or large or strangely shaped. Giving up is not an option for us, any more than it was for Jesus.

45

Losing Your Life
for the Gospel

8 : 35 – 38 & 9 : 1

For those who want to save their life will lose it, and those who
lose their life for my sake, and for the sake of the gospel, will save
it. For what will it profit them to gain the whole world and forfeit
their life? Indeed, what can they give in return for their life? Those
who are ashamed of me and of my words in this adulterous and
sinful generation, of them the Son of Man will also be ashamed
when he comes in the glory of his Father with the holy angels.'
And he said to them, 'Truly I tell you, there are some standing here
who will not taste death until they see that the kingdom of God
has come with power.'

SOME YEARS AGO I DESCRIBED HOW, AS A SMALL BOY, I HAD
become intrigued by the phrase 'Everyone is I', discovered in
one of the multitude of books that I read or ploughed through
without any guidance or discrimination at all during my childhood. The implications of that phrase staggered me. It was a
major revelation that each person on this planet is the star in
his or her own universe, and that the rest of us are nothing but
bit-players. We know so little about other people's lives because
we are so busy with our own. How does God cope with it?
How can he bear to see so many lives that he knows in such
intimate detail thrown away in return for the illusory benefits
of the world? How does he contain his anger and his
compassion?

There is no comparison, of course, but my mind is drawn to
an occasion, not so long ago, when I had come so close to the
life of a person other than myself that I began to feel crushed

by the weight of my own feelings. And what on earth is one to do with burdens that are too obscure to be properly or usefully shared? Of course, the potency of that question does not in any sense diminish the longing to be heard. Perhaps, I thought, it would be best to stop over-dramatising myself and simply tell someone. I decided to attempt the experiment. Results were poor. Mind you, I might have chosen the wrong time, place and person. It was in a church, during coffee-time after the service, the time when fellowship and spirituality flow into the vacuum created by the cessation of religion.

'What are you up to?' someone enquired.

'I'm up to two things,' I replied. 'I'm in the middle of writing a book, and that's hard, because getting usable ideas out of my head every morning is like hunting for blooms in the desert.'

This was not an entirely modest statement, I have to confess. If you search long and hard enough, you will find some particularly beautiful flowers wasting their sweetness on the desert air.

'Also,' I continued, 'I'm reading a book, and that's much more difficult. I'm about seven-eighths of the way through the collected letters of Oscar Wilde. It's been a very emotional experience.'

Are you familiar with a facial expression that combines puzzlement and ill-concealed scepticism?

'Why emotional?' asked the someone, with precisely that expression on his face.

I felt like some furry little nocturnal creature who has stuck his nose out during the day by mistake and been poked with a stick. My response was strategically untrue. I can't remember exactly what I said, some babbling nonsense about not having time to read nowadays, I expect. Whatever it was, it was a lie. My penance is to tell the truth now.

Reading such a book from beginning to end is like going on holiday with a person who everyone's heard of but no-one really knows. I wished I had arranged with a friend to read the book simultaneously. Some mutual off-loading would then have been possible. As it was I was in danger of becoming a Wilde bore. (That sentence sounds like some strange anthropomorphic miracle, doesn't it?) Already the eyes of my family and friends were glazing over whenever I began sentences with 'Did you know ...?'

Why so emotional?

First, there was something vaguely obscene about having access to every single surviving letter from one person. Correspondence, generally intended for the recipient only, was divested of its cloak of privacy and made available for comparison in a wholly unnatural way. Long letters to friends, telegrams, short notes, business matters, love letters, long-forgotten fragments, all displayed for me to goggle at. Manipulation, half-lies and heartfelt emotion, all laid bare. It felt like taking a man's brain apart with tweezers. My distaste for this naked epistolary parade was equalled only by the avidity with which, Hannibal Lecter-like, I devoured every word. Like many others, I am – have always been – fascinated by the life and works of this singular Victorian gentleman. Now, as I found myself reading on and on in every spare moment, I seemed to have been allowed a spare seat in the cockpit of his mind (or at least, in deference to the age in which he lived, a place in his carriage when he could afford one) as he drove and was driven towards disaster. As Oscar himself would have said, imagination is the quality that facilitates compassion. The experience of reading this book highlights that great Christian truth. Travelling that closely with Wilde or Raskolnikov has the same subversive effect on moral distinctions.

Let me share another aspect of the experience that deeply stirred my emotions. Put very simply, it was this. They are all dead, for goodness sake! All those people who received all those letters; every single man and woman so carefully identified in hundreds of footnotes, together with the years of birth and death in neat brackets, Oscar himself, his friends, his enemies, his wife, his children, his creditors, his contemporary admirers and critics, all have ceased to breathe and walk and talk and debate his life, this life and the life to come. I suppose it is inevitable, when one passes fifty, that such things can seem vitally important, and be deeply depressing. I was certainly affected like that, but, for me, the effect was ultimately not a negative one. I did feel a refreshment of my resolution to enjoy or use or relish or at least recognise the value of every God-given collection of twenty-four hours that remains in the rich account of my days.

My three week sojourn in Oscar's head (it really is a huge book!) produced another and equally significant determination in my heart. The question of whether the writer of these letters was a Christian is not one I or anyone else can answer on this side of the grave. *De Profundis*, his long, passionate letter written from prison to Alfred Douglas, contains stimulating and very moving references to the person and power of Jesus. Much of his writing (the fairytales and 'The Ballad of Reading Jail' are good examples) is saturated with an apprehension of the Spirit of God. Wilde flirted with the possibility of joining the Roman Catholic church throughout his life, and seems to have finally acquiesced in that connection on his deathbed. God knows the truth. He will sift through the damage and dross, and will retain all that is made of gold.

Recently, en-route to a more southerly destination, I found myself in Arques-la-Bataille, the village in Normandy where Wilde came on the first afternoon of his exile to France after release from prison. I sat, just as Oscar had done, on the battlements of the ancient and satisfyingly unmanicured castle that overlooks Arques, allowing my thoughts and feelings to roll across the valley like silent thunder. It was very good for me. It left me, not calm, but stabilised. It left me with a clear determination, as I emerged from such an intense and emotional involvement with the nuts and bolts of another's life, to renew my efforts to introduce Jesus to those who have not forsaken the pigs and followed the prodigal path to home. God sees, hears, reads every one of our communications, written, spoken and silent from the beginning of our lives to the end, and must weep even more copiously than I did as I read personal accounts of Oscar's death, when letters are the only things of any importance that remain.

What a sad and frightening image Jesus uses towards the end of this passage. The thought of Jesus being ashamed of me when he comes is almost too much to bear. Are you ever ashamed of him? Let me be honest. I have been sometimes. There have been moments when the whole creaky edifice of Christianity has so embarrassed me that I have come close to denying my involvement with it. Leaving aside the fact that that I have personally contributed to this creakiness, there is only one antidote for these feelings, and that is to do exactly what you and I are doing as we make our way through Mark's writings. We must go back to the one who is the pattern for the church. We must continually return to Jesus so that we can refresh our vision of who he is, what he is like and what he expects of us.

If we are serious about following Jesus there will be times when we feel like aliens in a strange land. Temptations to throw our lot in with the majority can be disturbingly strong. We must stay close to him.

46

The Transfiguration

9 : 2 – 13

Six days later, Jesus took with him Peter and James and John, and led them up a high mountain apart, by themselves. And he was transfigured before them, and his clothes became dazzling white, such as no one on earth could bleach them. And there appeared to them Elijah with Moses, who were talking with Jesus.

Then Peter said to Jesus, 'Rabbi, it is good for us to be here; let us make three dwellings, one for you, one for Moses, and one for Elijah.' He did not know what to say, for they were terrified.

Then a cloud overshadowed them, and from the cloud there came a voice, 'This is my Son, the Beloved; listen to him!' Suddenly when they looked around, they saw no one with them any more, but only Jesus.

As they were coming down the mountain, he ordered them to tell no one about what they had seen, until after the Son of Man had risen from the dead. So they kept the matter to themselves, questioning what this rising from the dead could mean.

Then they asked him, 'Why do the scribes say that Elijah must come first?'

He said to them, 'Elijah is indeed coming first to restore all things. How then is it written about the Son of Man, that he is to go through many sufferings and be treated with contempt? But I tell you that Elijah has come, and they did to him whatever they pleased, as it is written about him.'

HERE, AS BILL MURRAY SO MEMORABLY COMMENTED ABOUT something nearly as extraordinary but completely different in the film 'Ghostbusters', is something you don't see every day. A Kodak moment, if ever there was one. And that phrase is very appropriate in a way, because I have no doubt that in an age such as ours, Peter would have pulled his camera out of its bag and snapped foolishly away at the illustrious shining trio in an attempt to hide his terror and confusion. As it was, he came up with an idea that was interestingly similar. Perhaps, he suggested, the moment could be preserved by placing or enshrining each of these spiritual giants into the safely solid framework of a little dwelling or booth. It was an absurd suggestion, probably delivered in a high-pitched voice, but like so many of the absurd suggestions that I have made myself, it was born out of panic and fear. For all our yearning cries to God for 'something special' to happen, it can be very alarming when he hears us, and something does.

In the two thousand years since God became man, whole

sections of the church have been seriously impoverished by this tendency to separate spiritual from earthly reality by putting the former into some sort of artificial frame. The attempt to distance ourselves from the dazzling immanence of God by depositing it in structures made from times or rhymes or words or stone or wood is very understandable, sometimes useful, and often very interesting and beautiful. In the final analysis, though, it needs to be our hearts and minds that constitute the framework within which the Holy Spirit lives and moves. The shining must not be upon us, so that we are seen, but from within us, so that Jesus is visible.

A sobering moment for Jesus recorded in the last part of this passage. After the poignancy and power of his mountain-top experience the disciples' questions lead him to reflect on the fact that, just as his cousin John has taken the Elijah role and suffered and died as a consequence, so he too has embarked on a road that can lead only to pain, contempt and death. That knowledge was always there, nagging at him like the worst toothache in the history of the world.

47

The Healing of a Boy with a Spirit

9 : 14 – 29

When they came to the disciples, they saw a great crowd around them, and some scribes arguing with them. When the whole crowd saw him, they were immediately overcome with awe, and they ran forward to greet him.

He asked them, 'What are you arguing about with them?'

Someone from the crowd answered him, 'Teacher, I brought

you my son; he has a spirit that makes him unable to speak; and whenever it seizes him, it dashes him down; and he foams and grinds his teeth and becomes rigid; and I asked your disciples to cast it out, but they could not do so.'

He answered them, 'You faithless generation, how much longer must I be among you? How much longer must I put up with you? Bring him to me.' And they brought the boy to him.

When the spirit saw him, immediately it convulsed the boy, and he fell on the ground and rolled about, foaming at the mouth. Jesus asked the father, 'How long has this been happening to him?' And he said, 'From childhood. It has often cast him into the fire and into the water, to destroy him; but if you are able to do anything, have pity on us and help us.'

Jesus said to him, 'If you are able! – All things can be done for the one who believes.'

Immediately the father of the child cried out, 'I believe; help my unbelief!'

When Jesus saw that a crowd came running together, he rebuked the unclean spirit, saying to it, 'You spirit that keeps this boy from speaking and hearing, I command you, come out of him, and never enter him again!' After crying out and convulsing him terribly, it came out, and the boy was like a corpse, so that most of them said, 'He is dead.'

But Jesus took him by the hand and lifted him up, and he was able to stand. When he had entered the house, his disciples asked him privately, 'Why could we not cast it out?'

He said to them, 'This kind can come out only through prayer.'

WHAT WERE THE SCRIBES AND THE CROWD AND THE disciples arguing about? We may presume that the disciples, who had latterly enjoyed exercising the power invested in them by Jesus, had ended up, scarlet-faced, in a very embarrassing situation where nothing they pronounced or did made any difference to the state of this severely afflicted lad. I wonder what they said when faced with failure. Did they make excuses? Did they try to remain cool and look as if they knew exactly why things weren't going according to plan? Did they come up with a list of possible explanations to appease the father and shut the scribes up? Those scribes must have loved it, mustn't they? Here were these followers of the so-called Messiah making complete idiots of themselves in front of a large crowd. Just what they'd been looking for. Excellent!

Then Jesus arrives.

The poor father, his faith obviously eroded by the failure he has been witnessing, cries out in desperation about the terrible epilepsy-like fits that have nearly brought about his son's death over the years. As usual, exasperation turns to compassion as Jesus witnesses the pitiful state of the young man, perceives the depth of grief in his father, and hears that tearful request to be given more faith. The boy is healed, of course.

Later, in private (you bet your sweet life it was in private!) the disciples ask Jesus why they were unable to heal the boy. He explains that this particular kind of spirit can only be removed, as far as they are concerned, by prayer, or prayer and fasting, as some manuscripts have it.

The lessons from this fascinating record are valuable for us as a church.

First, when something goes wrong or we seem to have failed in the sight of others, and especially unbelievers, let's for goodness sake be honest and open about our ignorance. We can trust that Jesus will have the answer, and that he will do whatever is right and necessary. As soon as we start to make excuses and invent reasons for our failure we run the risk of repelling those who might have been attracted by our personal vulnerability.

Secondly, it is clear from this account that there is more than one way to approach healing. I may be very fond of the neat little theories that I have developed, but God knows what is actually needed and I must always be ready to learn and adapt.

Thirdly, this story has given us one of the greatest, simplest prayers of all time. 'I believe, help my unbelief.' I pray it all the time.

48

Jesus Again Foretells His Death and Resurrection

9 : 30 – 32

They went on from there and passed through Galilee. He did not want anyone to know it; for he was teaching his disciples, saying to them, 'The Son of Man is to be betrayed into human hands, and they will kill him, and three days after being killed, he will rise again.' But they did not understand what he was saying and were afraid to ask him.

WERE THEY AFRAID BECAUSE HE MIGHT GET ANGRY WITH them, or were they afraid because they didn't like all this talk of death? Whatever the reason, their fear and lack of response can only have heightened feelings of loneliness and apprehension in Jesus. He knew that he was going to die an early death, and there must have been times when that knowledge weighed upon him like a stone, especially as he was the only one who understood why it was necessary.

Death is a terrible prospect for most of us, if we are honest. Christians have a hope and a belief that Jesus has defeated death, but to a lesser or greater extent the fear of leaving this life and plunging into the unknown troubles all of us.

Two things spring to mind as I think about this. The first is a scene from 'Measure for Measure' by William Shakespeare. One of the main characters, Claudio, has been condemned to death, and is visited by his sister Isabella who is about to enter a nunnery. Isabella reveals to Claudio that his life could be saved if she were to agree to sacrifice her chastity to Angelo, who, as deputy for the absent Duke of Vienna proclaimed the death sentence on Claudio. Isabella offers her brother this news purely as information. She is sure that her brother's sense of honour would never allow him to agree to such an arrangement. In this she is disappointed. The terror of death drives out all other considerations.

CLAUDIO: Death is a fearful thing.
ISABELLA: And shamed life a hateful.
CLAUDIO: Ay, but to die, and go we know not where;
To lie in cold obstruction, and to rot;
This sensible warm motion to become
A kneaded clod, and the dilated spirit
To bathe in fiery floods, or to reside
In thrilling region of thick-ribbed ice;
To be imprisoned in the viewless winds,
And blown with restless violence round about
The pendent world; or to be worse than worst
Of those that lawless and incertain thought
Imagine howling – 'tis too horrible!
The weariest and most loathed worldly life
That age, ache, penury and imprisonment
Can lay on nature is a paradise
To what we fear of death.
ISABELLA: Alas, alas!
CLAUDIO: Sweet sister, let me live …

The other thing that I thought of was an extract from 'Ghosts', the book that I wrote before this one. The main character, David Herrick, is unable to come to terms with the early and unexpected death of his wife. Walking the hills with an old friend called Jenny, he responds emotionally to her suggestion that, one day, he will see Jessica in heaven.

'I don't want to see her in heaven. I want to see her *now*! I don't want her to become something that isn't properly human. Something bright and unphysical and non-confrontational and angelic. I don't want to be met by her in thirty or forty years at the gates of heaven smiling ethereally at me and telling me to come farther in and farther up or anything like that. I have never hated all things mystical as much as I hate them now. I want walks in the wood and having to wash your wellies afterwards. I want trips to the supermarket and arguments over what we're going to do at weekends and underwear hanging in the bathroom and discussions about who could possibly own the originless dead-toad shoes that always seemed to collect in our porch and getting into bed together and one of us having to get up again because we've forgotten to lock the back door, and hands and touch and food and clothes and Christmas and talking about people and – and praying together about the future.'

A lying pair of magpies flew overhead, pirates looking for plunder on a freezing, foodless day. I lowered my head, sighing heavily.

'The dead have to give up their membership cards, don't they, Jenny? They can never belong again. Willing or unwilling, they've gone pioneering off to the next stage, changed by the very act of exploration into beings who have no place with us and our weather and our pubs and our feeble attempts to say what we feel. How can they do that to us? How can they?' I smiled bleakly as Jenny spontaneously took my arm and laid her face comfortingly against the sleeve of my coat. 'Yes, of course you're right. Jessica has gone to be with Jesus, and thank God for that. Just at present, though, I can't rid myself of the notion that they've both done a lot better out of the deal than me. Don't worry.' I placed an arm around her shoulders and patted her reassuringly. 'It'll all get sorted out, but there's no point kidding myself. I've got a long way to go.'

Jesus was no Claudio, of course. For him, there was never any question of moral compromise. Nor could he have been unaware of the ineffable pleasures that reunion with his Father in heaven would bring. Nevertheless, as a human being, the prospect of inevitable pain and death must have brought him to a very low state at times. We all have a long way to go when it comes to dealing with the idea of death, but, as usual, Jesus was there first.

49

Who Is the Greatest?

9 : 33 – 37
(and have a look at Matthew 25 : 31 – 46)

Then they came to Capernaum; and when he was in the house he asked them, 'What were you arguing about on the way?'

But they were silent, for on the way they had argued with one another who was the greatest. He sat down, called the twelve, and said to them, 'Whoever wants to be first must be last of all and servant of all.' Then he took a little child and put it among them; and taking it in his arms, he said to them, 'Whoever welcomes one such child in my name welcomes me, and whoever welcomes me welcomes not me but the one who sent me.'

THERE IS NOT A MORE TEDIOUSLY ORTHODOX CHRISTIAN than me under the sun, or the rain, or any other weather you care to name. I believe that there is only one way to eternal life, only one route to the Father who loves us, and that is Jesus. He is the way and the truth and the life. So that's that – sort of.

When Bridget and I visited the distant, poverty-stricken country of Bangladesh (I shall say more about that later in this book), the most impressive piece of work we witnessed was a programme to help the street-girls who exist, homeless and loveless, in the middle of some of the worst slums in the world. This programme, financed and administered by the aid agency World Vision, gives these sad, confused little people a chance to experience order, cleanliness, normal play, kindness and hope for the future, often for the first time in their lives. It was run by two women, one a Christian and the other a Muslim. These two ladies are absolutely dedicated to their work, but they will never write paperback testimony books for mass consumption, or speak to large crowds in big tents at international festivals, or sign Bibles for admirers. They are too busy doing the job.

I have an idea about this little Muslim lady who has picked so many filthy children up from the garbage-strewn streets of Dhaka. My idea is that when she meets Jesus she might look at him with curiosity and wonder in her eyes and say, 'Oh, it's you! I met you so *many* times, but I can't quite remember ...'

And Jesus will gently explain, 'You took me from the street when I was hungry and homeless. You fed me and clothed me and gave me hope when I was in despair.'

Then she will cry, 'But, Lord, I am the least of persons. When did I do all these things for you?'

'When you did it for just one of those little children,' he will reply, 'you did it for me. When you welcomed each one of them, you welcomed me. And now, I welcome you.'

That's my idea. I could be wrong of course.

50

Another Exorcist

9 : 38 – 41

John said to him, 'Teacher, we saw someone casting out demons in your name, and we tried to stop him, because he was not following us.'

But Jesus said, 'Do not stop him; for no one who does a deed of power in my name will be able soon afterward to speak evil of me. Whoever is not against us is for us. For truly I tell you, whoever gives you a cup of water to drink because you bear the name of Christ will by no means lose the reward.

THERE IS AN INTERESTING LITTLE PRINCIPLE HIDDEN AWAY IN the centre of this passage, and it has a much wider application than one might think. Jesus says that a person who does deeds of power in his name will not be able to speak evil of him soon afterwards. Anyone who has worked with groups of children will know exactly what this means. Quite often, during the years when Bridget and I were working with teenage children in all sorts of different situations, we found that giving very difficult children a special responsibility was helpful in moderating their behaviour towards us and the rest of the group. Of course, you have to be careful with this sort of thing. The aim is certainly not to reward bad behaviour, but to involve the person concerned in the nuts and bolts of what is happening, to help them feel that they have an investment in the success or failure of the lesson or project or activity.

The principle holds good in church as well. In its more shallow manifestation, I have noticed that if I do the talk or the prayers or the reading on a Sunday I am much more likely to take an alert interest in the rest of the service. Not very impressive, is it? But that is, by and large, the way in which human beings work. Much more importantly, it is also true that involvement can allow uncertain church attenders to move from a sense of inadequacy to a feeling that they really do have something to contribute to the corporate well-being of the church community.

A friend called Anne who stayed with us last year, for instance, was telling us that she had never remotely considered the prospect of leading worship in her church. By preference she was a 'back row' Christian, and she had always felt slightly detached from things that happened at the front or in the body of the church. Then, one day, someone buttonholed her during coffee-time after the service.

'I think you'd make a very good worship leader,' said this person with little or no preamble.

Anne was a little shocked. She had never seen herself in that role, and was fairly sure she never would. As the weeks went by, though, those few words of encouragement nagged at her attention. Surely she *couldn't*. But then, maybe she could! How would she ever know if she never tried? She talked to the minister, and a couple of weeks later, in great fear and trembling, led worship for the first time. Not only did she do it well, she enjoyed it, and that Sunday marked the beginning of a change in her life and her faith. She was assisting the congregation in moving closer to the heart of God, and it was impossible for her not be moved and altered in the process. It is amazing what people can do when you give them a chance.

As a footnote to this passage, here is a silly little secret of mine. On becoming a Christian when I was a teenager I found myself very impressed by this business of the gift of a cup of water earning its reward. Sometimes, when people did things for me I tried to find a way to let them know that I was a Christian. If, knowing that, they repeated the gift, then, I reasoned, they must be in line for a reward. Nowadays I don't believe God is as legalistic as that, but still, if there is a way of doing it without sounding completely mad, I do like to let people know that God smiles on their kindness.

51

Temptations to Sin

9 : 42 – 50

'If any of you put a stumbling block before one of these little ones who believe in me, it would be better for you if a great millstone were hung around your neck and you were thrown into the sea. If your hand causes you to stumble, cut it off; it is better for you to enter life maimed than to have two hands and to go to hell, to the unquenchable fire. And if your foot causes you to stumble, cut it off; it is better for you to enter life lame than to have two feet and to be thrown into hell. And if your eye causes you to stumble, tear it out; it is better for you to enter the kingdom of God with one eye

than to have two eyes and to be thrown into hell, where their
worm never dies, and the fire is never quenched.

'For everyone will be salted with fire. Salt is good; but if salt
has lost its saltiness, how can you season it? Have salt in yourselves, and be at peace with one another.'

I AM AMAZED THAT THESE VERSES HAVE NOT SPAWNED A SECT
whose members make a point of chopping bits of themselves
off every time a part of their body causes them to sin. Perhaps I
am wrong and there actually is such a sect, but lack of physical
equipment has made it impossible for them to communicate their
existence. After all, if we were to take Jesus literally, there wouldn't
be much left of most of us, would there? The mind boggles!

What is Jesus talking about?

I think he is talking about denial. More than that, he is talking about a level of denial that can leave us feeling as if an
essential part of ourselves has been removed. In the case of
Jesus himself the list writes itself. Some examples. He was never
to marry and have children. As we have already seen from that
famous moment when he turned on Peter, he could not indulge
in the comfort of friends when that comfort was likely to draw
him from the path of duty. In the prime of his life he voluntarily
abandoned the sweetly granular joys of living in order that his
death should make eternal life possible for us. These decisions
must have been like amputations, mustn't they? He was not
able to have these things *sometimes* or just a *little* bit. They
were options that quite simply had to be removed as an arm or
a leg is removed. No doubt, as with those who have suffered
physical amputations, the pain in the phantom limb could be
excruciating at times.

As for us, Jesus is saying very clearly here that it is very
dangerous for the souls of us men and women when we wilfully
retain elements or features of our lives that result in sin, especially when they also cause others to sin. What sorts of things
might he be referring to? Well, you know as well as I do really.
Things like that cosily developing relationship that is giving

130

you all the old exciting feelings of being alive and in love, but with a person who is not your wife or husband. Cut it off, says Jesus. Yes, it will hurt, of course it will. But you must cut it off for the sake of yourself and the other people who will eventually be affected. Unhealthy addictions, crooked means of making money, subtle neglect, chronic laziness – the list, significantly, is as long as that dispensable arm of yours.

52

Teaching about Divorce

10 : 1 – 12

He left that place and went to the region of Judea and beyond the Jordan. And crowds again gathered around him; and, as was his custom, he again taught them. Some Pharisees came, and to test him they asked, 'Is it lawful for a man to divorce his wife?'

He answered them, 'What did Moses command you?'

They said, 'Moses allowed a man to write a certificate of dismissal and to divorce her.'

But Jesus said to them, 'Because of your hardness of heart he wrote this commandment for you. But from the beginning of creation, "God made them male and female." "For this reason a man shall leave his father and mother and be joined to his wife, and the two shall become one flesh." So they are no longer two, but one flesh. Therefore what God has joined together, let no one separate.'

Then in the house the disciples asked him again about this matter. He said to them, 'Whoever divorces his wife and marries another commits adultery against her; and if she divorces her husband and marries another, she commits adultery.'

I BELIEVE A VITAL LESSON CAN BE LEARNED FROM THIS PASSAGE, quite apart from the issues connected with marriage and divorce. But you may find that you disagree with me about the exact nature of that lesson.

When I was a young man and an even younger Christian, I belonged to a Bible-study group that met on Wednesdays. Memory tells me that the group was made up of a few middle-aged ladies with rather low opinions of themselves, a flippant youth who drove everyone mad, a nice elderly fellow who said little and didn't need to, a married couple with a real gift for hospitality who were the leaders of the group, myself, and one other man (I shall call him Percy) who had a great deal to say and tended to support his opinions with references from the writings of the Old Testament. Any attempt to argue with this means of justification was met with the retort that Jesus himself frequently quoted from the Old Testament, and if it was good enough for him it should be good enough for us.

Thus, for instance, we were bound to be in favour of capital punishment, according to Percy.

'Read Leviticus,' said Percy trenchantly. 'That was God's way in those days, wasn't it, and we're surely not saying that God changes, are we?'

At this point we would all miserably nod or shake our heads, then abruptly switch from nodding to shaking or shaking to nodding as we wrestled with the assorted grammar of Percy's purely rhetorical question.

I suppose we were a mild and slightly troubled group, and we knew very little about the Bible. If we had been more knowledgeable we might have asked Percy if he thought that children who disobeyed their parents should be taken outside the city and stoned to death, or thrown into bear pits if they were cheeky to older men with bald heads (like Percy). Were we to stick with 'an eye for an eye and a tooth for a tooth' and ignore the teachings of Jesus about forgiveness?

I wish I had known Percy in the later part of my life. There is much I would like to have said to him. He has gone now. I do hope he is not doomed to spend eternity at the gates of heaven haranguing a polite but weary angel about his entitlement to enter on the basis of some tediously obscure verse in the Pentateuch.

In more recent years those who espouse the so-called health-and-wealth movement are able to point to Old Testament scriptures that do indeed promise riches and good fortune to those who walk closely with their God.

'Look,' they say, just as Percy used to, 'it's in the Bible. You can't argue with that! Well, can you?'

No, you can't. It *is* in the Bible. And yes, Jesus *did* frequently quote the Old Testament. And, no, of course God doesn't change.

But the passage we have just read is in the Bible as well, and the person who speaks these words is the Living Word, the clearest, purest, most accurate image or picture of God that we will encounter on this side of heaven. And what is he saying to these Percys – I mean – these Pharisees? He is saying that Moses allowed divorce as a temporary concession, but that the true will of God is for marriages to be permanent. And he is implying much more than that. He is showing them (and us) with great clarity that the teaching of the past must be viewed through the revelation of the true nature of God in Jesus.

We ignore the Old Testament at our peril. It records the dealings of God with man, and the words that it uses are given to us by God. But we are followers of Jesus. We know that our master came to uphold every tittle and jot of the law, but we also know that he came to fulfil it. Without compromising his commitment to the law in the least, he found a way to rescue the woman taken in adultery – and you and me if it comes to that. Grace can do bewildering tricks with the law. Let's be careful.

My views on divorce?

God hates divorce, but not quite as much as he hates the inability or refusal of some Christians to forgive and gracefully receive those whose lives have been torn apart by conflict and cruelty and pain. That's my view.

53

Jesus Blesses Little Children

10 : 13 – 16

People were bringing little children to him in order that he might touch them; and the disciples spoke sternly to them. But when Jesus saw this, he was indignant and said to them, 'Let the little children come to me; do not stop them; for it is to such as these that the kingdom of God belongs. Truly I tell you, whoever does not receive the kingdom of God as a little child will never enter it.' And he took them up in his arms, laid his hands on them, and blessed them.

A S I READ THIS PASSAGE FOR THE THOUSANDTH TIME I remember many Christians I have known whose sincere desire to follow Jesus has been impeded by a Christian upbringing. Let me explain such a foolish-sounding paradox.

Perhaps the most obvious examples of this phenomenon occur in denominations and Christian groups whose adherents have developed what we might describe as a tribal approach to life in the church and at home. Dress, behaviour, language, social interaction and general world-view have been so solidly established over generations that children simply grow into the shape prescribed for them by the religious community to which they belong. Some of the groupings in our own islands are, sadly, clear examples of this, but all denominations and Christian gatherings are vulnerable to the temptation of making camp at the roadside, as it were, instead of following Jesus on into unknown and possibly perilous places.

A friend described how, as a teenager in her particular church, the evils of dancing, cinema and 'unsuitable' music were emphasised constantly to her. So strongly were these terrible things preached against, that, for her, the Christian faith was defined by the need to avoid such dangerous pitfalls. Jesus, who replaced ten commandments featuring a lot about what you shouldn't do with two commandments about what you must do, hardly figured in her thinking.

'The problem is,' said my friend, 'that the child in me still believes all the silly things I was taught, even though my mind rejects them and wants to move on.'

And, of course, that is true of much that we learned as children, isn't it? I can think of examples in my own life.

I have mentioned elsewhere, for instance, that I still find it difficult to believe I can go and buy a new tin of shoe-polish if I want to. My memory is of there being only the one tin in our house throughout my childhood. The business of vigorously gouging and scraping one more scrap of polish from the grooves around the rim of this permanently exhausted container was a daily battle. New tin? Huh! Never was such a thing. Never will be.

Then there was Wimbledon. I used to watch the BBC coverage of the Wimbledon tennis fortnight on our black-and-white television set. Why, I wondered, was the person at the far end of the court given the advantage of playing downhill, while his poor opponent at the near end had to hit the ball extra hard to get the ball to the top of the slope. As I watched my first match from the edge of a real tennis court, there was a part of me that found it hard to accept the way in which they had flattened the courts since the days when it was perfectly clear to me that they had a gradient of about one in four.

I shared G. K. Chesterton's boyhood belief that the movement of the trees created the wind, and not the other way round. Every now and then the trees at the end of our garden would decide to give the sky a good thrashing. In the process they could cause anything from a breeze to a howling gale. I greeted attempts to correct this impression with deep scepticism. The evidence was before my eyes. It still is.

Speaking of trees, as a small child I knew without any shadow of doubt that silver-birches were made of solid silver. I dreamed of cutting through one with a saw and running my fingers over the cold, shining metal surfaces that would be revealed. There were three silver-birches in our garden. We were rich. If all else failed we could chop them into slices and sell the pieces for a fortune. Silver logs. As an adult I still know deep inside myself that they are made of that precious metal.

My father told me often that if I pulled faces I would 'stay like it'. The thought haunted me for years. I kept my face as expressionless as possible. I still do. If I were to laugh or frown – good heavens! – I might stay like it.

Yes, the things we knew as children may turn out to be factually incorrect, but that is a mere detail. They are true for ever.

And that is why Jesus insists here, as he holds a child gently in his arms, that we must receive him like little children if we wish to enter the Kingdom of God. On the day when we first meet him, or later on if we are like my friend, who didn't or couldn't get round to it when she should have done, we say these words to him:

'Lord Jesus, as far as I am able, I bring myself before you as an ignorant child. I want to be a blank sheet of paper. I set aside all that I thought I knew, every one of my carefully cultivated beliefs and convictions and principles, and I wait for you to fill me with a truth that will last for ever.'

54

The Rich Man

10 : 17 – 31

As he was setting out on a journey, a man ran up and knelt before him, and asked him, 'Good Teacher, what must I do to inherit eternal life?' Jesus said to him, 'Why do you call me good? No one is good but God alone. You know the commandments: "You shall not murder; You shall not commit adultery; You shall not steal; You shall not bear false witness; You shall not defraud; Honour your father and mother." '

He said to him, 'Teacher, I have kept all these since my youth.'

Jesus, looking at him, loved him and said, 'You lack one thing; go, sell what you own, and give the money to the poor, and you will have treasure in heaven; then come, follow me.'

When he heard this, he was shocked and went away grieving, for he had many possessions. Then Jesus looked around and said to his disciples, 'How hard it will be for those who have wealth to enter the kingdom of God!'

And the disciples were perplexed at these words.

But Jesus said to them again, 'Children, how hard it is to enter the kingdom of God! It is easier for a camel to go through the eye of a needle than for someone who is rich to enter the kingdom of God.'

They were greatly astounded and said to one another, 'Then who can be saved?'

Jesus looked at them and said, 'For mortals it is impossible, but not for God; for God all things are possible.'

Peter began to say to him, 'Look, we have left everything and followed you.'

Jesus said, 'Truly I tell you, there is no one who has left house or brothers or sisters or mother or father or children or fields, for my sake and for the sake of the good news, who will not receive a hundredfold now in this age – houses, brothers and sisters, mothers and children, and fields with persecutions – and in the age to come eternal life. But many who are first will be last, and the last will be first.'

QUITE APART FROM ANYTHING ELSE THIS FAMOUS EPISODE might be regarded as a parable concerning the responsibilities of rich Christians in places like Great Britain towards the millions who live at starvation level in other parts of the world.

We are told that this man, a young man according to the account in Matthew's gospel, was shocked by Jesus' suggestion that he should sell all that he had, and it really is very easy to understand why. It is a fact of life that the identity we cobble together for ourselves is largely defined by what we have or do, and by the way in which other people see us. The shock was produced by Jesus saying, in effect, that having been a genuinely good person within the safe and comfortable setting of a rich lifestyle, this chap who so wanted eternal life should shift his security base from money and all that it could buy, to Jesus. It must have been like looking at his reflection and discovering that someone had substituted a distorting mirror for the normal one. The hypothetical image that Jesus reflected back to this earnest young man was just too different and difficult for him to handle. He went away crying because he simply could not bring himself to take the step that Jesus was asking for. He was not able to redefine himself to that extent. I do hope he went on to make the right decision at some later date.

We are so very rich in countries like this, aren't we? When I offer that view to people it can provoke a variety of responses. Some simply agree. Many people do give regularly without saying much about it. Others tell me that it's all relative, that there is much more poverty in our own country than we realise, and that charity begins at home. Some say they would give, but that they don't trust the aid agencies or the people who initially receive the money or goods in the countries concerned. They are not prepared to risk their hard-earned cash disappearing into the pockets of those who don't need it. Others simply express a weariness with the whole business of poverty and the way in which advertising campaigns play on emotions in such a way that they either give reluctantly and feel guilty, or don't give at all and feel even more guilty.

I can identify with these responses. At one time or another I have felt them all. I have already mentioned Bangladesh in this book. Everything changed back at the beginning of 2000 when my wife and I visited that country to meet the child we had sponsored through the aid agency, World Vision, and to collect material for a fund-raising book. In the slums of Dhaka tired old religious arguments collapse like badly made shelves falling off walls. There are millions of children and adults struggling to survive in that soaked and battered country. We were able to witness a little of the problem for ourselves. It was enough to change us for ever.

Included in the presentation we toured with on our return was a sketch that sums it all up. It features a crooked time-share agent confronted with one of his customers who is far from happy with the time-share she has bought into. Not surprising, as her 'holiday home' is set in the slums of Dhaka.

'C' is the customer and 'A' is the agent.

C: Morning! Remember me, Mr Finn?

A: Of course, Mrs Smith. You wisely invested in one of our Bangladeshi time-share options. One of our lucky customers.

C: Oh, do you have *lucky* customers? No, I'm not one of them.

A: Not – lucky?

C: No, Mr Finn, neither wise nor lucky. I've just spent a fortnight at the house you sold me a share in. I thought I'd pop in and show you my holiday snaps..

A: Oh! That's nice. Did it go well? Or …

C: Mr Finn, you said my house was set in a popular suburb of the city of Dhaka.

A: Well, isn't it?

C: Oh, yes, very popular. Five million people live there. You described it as, and I quote, 'discreetly distanced from the hustle and bustle of city life and refreshingly free from all garish excesses and extravagances of the modern urban life-style'.

A: Yes, well, it is. It is a – it's a …

C: Slum – is the word you're groping for, Mr Finn. You sold me a house in a slum, didn't you?

A: Well, it depends how you define 'slum'.

C: Oh, right. So, you think between a comfortable, fully equipped holiday villa in a beautiful resort, and a smelly, broken-down shack in the middle of a slum in the

poorest country in the world, there's a sort of grey area
that makes telling the difference a bit tricky?

A: Well -

C: Look at this photo, Mr Finn. There's my house – see – in
the centre. Now, your brochure mentioned an 'integrated
garden feature'. Would that be this tree growing up
through the roof?

A: Err, yes, yes, that's it ...

C: And here's a close-up of my house. You reassured me
that, at most, it might need 'a spot of sympathetic
refurbishment'.

A: Ah, mm -

C: It has no walls. No walls, Mr Finn! In what sense *is* this a
house? Just how sympathetic do I need to get?

A: Nice and airy when the sun -

C: Now, unless I'm very much mistaken, in this shot of my
house, we see your 'perpendicular flood evasion system'.
Meaning?

A: Well, you climb up on the err -

C: The roof. And in the same picture I suspect we are seeing
examples of the 'Economy, elevated solar laundry
facility'. Right?

A: Err, yes, you lay your washing out on the err -

C: On the perpendicular flood evasion system, yes. Speaking
of which, presumably the vast sheet of water I found
behind the slums is your 'Climatically adjusted, annual
water feature'. Those are floods, Mr Finn. They come
every year. Ah! Perhaps that would be the 'seasonal
opportunity for underwater sports' mentioned in your
literature?

A: Well, yes -

C: And could this picture of people washing their clothes in
the ditch at the side of the street possibly be an
illustration of the 'Alfresco community utility area'?

A: Well, that's what those ditches are for. That's what they
do in them.

C: That's not all they do in them. And what's this pile of
rubbish at the side of the road?

A: The oxygenated garbage recycling procedure.

C: You mean it rots in the open air, don't you?

A: Well, yes.

C: I thought so. And 'bio-degradable'?

A: Covered in flies.

C: And what is this?

A: Oh, this is the 'Random aperture, ceiling mounted air-conditioning feature, incorporating a free water-sprinkling system in case of fire'.

C: Wrong. This is a rusty old bit of corrugated iron with holes in it that constitutes the roof of the so-called house you sold me. The whole thing's a disaster, Mr Finn!

A: Look, I must have got *something* right! I said it was 'compact'.

C: Eight foot square.

A: 'Rock-bottom power bills'?

C: No power.

A: 'Unbreakable windows'?

C: No glass.

A: 'Natural-look floor-covering'?

C: Mud. (PAUSE) What have you got to say about all this, Mr Finn?

A: (PAUSE) Errm – going back next year ...?

Of course – Jesus says it himself in this passage – being rich does not make it impossible to enter the Kingdom of Heaven, and many wealthy people do an enormous amount of good by dealing effectively and productively with the money available to them. But if we profess to be followers of Jesus, we had better hold our wealth with a very loose grip indeed, and remember those who have nothing. Incidentally, those who understand the money markets should check out the rate that Jesus offers in this passage for those who make sacrifices for him. A guaranteed, one hundred per-cent return on your investment, and no tax! What are you waiting for?

55

A Third Time Jesus Foretells His Death and Resurrection

10 : 32 – 34

They were on the road, going up to Jerusalem, and Jesus was walking ahead of them; they were amazed, and those who followed
were afraid.

He took the twelve aside again and began to tell them what
was to happen to him, saying, 'See, we are going up to Jerusalem,
and the Son of Man will be handed over to the chief priests and
the scribes, and they will condemn him to death; then they will
hand him over to the Gentiles; they will mock him, and spit upon
him, and flog him, and kill him; and after three days he will rise
again.'

A RESPECTED MODERN THEOLOGIAN SAYS THAT IF WE DO NOT
believe Jesus ever doubted his own divinity, we have not
understood the gospels at all.

He will rise again
But what of me?
Though death flaps down to take me like a huge black bird
Casting ragged shadows over lilies of the valley
Over milky moonlit seas
Sunrise glory
Sunset flame
Peach and pearl in Galilean skies
The coolness of a woman's hand
Children's eyes
The rasp of rough-grained wood against the skin

Light in the gaze of men, who, by a miracle of faith, have
      seen
Heard, walked, talked
Discovered that their pitted skin is whole and clean
Sabbath walks, meandering through rolling fields of wheat
The chattering and chuckling of my friends
Their sweet naïveté
A scent of cooking fish
The call to eat
Old stories by the fire
Good wine
A kiss
Love and wisdom in my mother's smile
The tears of those who loved me much
Because I gently, fiercely took away their sin
And will I rise again?
Indeed, the son of man must rise and live once more
But what of me?
What of me?

56

The Request of
James and John

10 : 35 – 45

James and John, the sons of Zebedee, came forward to him and
said to him, 'Teacher, we want you to do for us whatever we ask
of you.'

And he said to them, 'What is it you want me to do for you?'

And they said to him, 'Grant us to sit, one at your right hand
and one at your left, in your glory.'

But Jesus said to them, 'You do not know what you are asking.

Are you able to drink the cup that I drink, or be baptized with the baptism that I am baptized with?'

They replied, 'We are able.'

Then Jesus said to them, 'The cup that I drink you will drink; and with the baptism with which I am baptized, you will be baptized; but to sit at my right hand or at my left is not mine to grant, but it is for those for whom it has been prepared.'

When the ten heard this, they began to be angry with James and John. So Jesus called them and said to them, 'You know that among the Gentiles those whom they recognize as their rulers lord it over them, and their great ones are tyrants over them. But it is not so among you; but whoever wishes to become great among you must be your servant, and whoever wishes to be first among you must be slave of all. For the Son of Man came not to be served but to serve, and to give his life a ransom for many.'

H OW LONG DO YOU THINK IT TOOK JAMES AND JOHN TO work up the nerve to ask this question. Imagine the discussion beforehand:

JAMES: Look, let's not just come straight out with it, eh?

JOHN: What do you mean?

JAMES: Well, we don't want him to say no straightaway, do we? Let's begin by asking him if he'll give us whatever it is we want before we actually tell him what it is, then if he says he will we'll know we're going to get what we want, whatever it is.

JOHN: Mmmm, sounds sort of clever enough. Trouble is, you know what he's like. He sometimes knows what we're thinking before we say something completely different, doesn't he?

JAMES: Yes, but not always. Sometimes he doesn't, especially when you think he might.

JOHN: True, yes that's true. He might get very angry when we do get round to asking him, though. I mean, he does get angry, doesn't he?

JAMES: Oh, he does, he does – but not always, and usually when you're not really expecting it.

JOHN: True. Right. Right. So, what it boils down to is this.
         If we do our very best to expect him to know what
         we're thinking before we say it and to be really angry
         with us for saying it – or rather thinking it if we
         never get the chance to say it – then he probably
         won't.

JAMES: Won't what?

JOHN: I'm not sure. I've got a bit confused. I don't even
         know what *I'm* thinking.

JAMES: Oh, never mind! I'll do the talking, you just keep
         your mind as blank as possible. Shouldn't be a
         problem. By the way, just before we start, you do
         know your right from your left, do you?

JOHN: Ah, I was going to ask you about that. Are we
         talking about seats to his left and right as you face
         him in glory, or are we talking about, as it were,
         stage left and stage right – you know, looking from
         behind, in the same direction as him?

JAMES: Does that actually matter?

JOHN: Err, not really, no. It's just – for afterwards when I
         tell my mum. You know, she always wants the details
         …

Reading between the lines of the actual recorded conversation, there is the suggestion of a rather touching blend of
amusement and sadness in the response of Jesus to these close
lieutenants of his. Can you see a smile playing around his lips
as he sees through their naïve opening gambit and asks them
what it is that they want? On hearing their request he tells them
that they have no idea what he himself must go through before
returning to glory, and then, in a sudden sad vision of the
future, he sees that these two beloved disciples of his must also
suffer a terrible death before being reunited with him. In any
case, Jesus concludes, perhaps avoiding a more complex and
temporarily meaningless reply, such privileges are not his to
give.

Later, tackling the root of their motivation for approaching him, he explains to all of his disciples that the desire for reward and recognition will get them nowhere. Be a slave to all and you will achieve greatness. That was the message to his disciples then, and that is the message to his disciples now.

57

The Healing
of Blind Bartimaeus

10 : 46 – 52

They came to Jericho. As he and his disciples and a large crowd were leaving Jericho, Bartimaeus son of Timaeus, a blind beggar, was sitting by the roadside. When he heard that it was Jesus of Nazareth, he began to shout out and say, 'Jesus, Son of David, have mercy on me!' Many sternly ordered him to be quiet, but he cried out even more loudly, 'Son of David, have mercy on me!' Jesus stood still and said, 'Call him here.' And they called the blind man, saying to him, 'Take heart; get up, he is calling you.' So throwing off his cloak, he sprang up and came to Jesus. Then Jesus said to him, 'What do you want me to do for you?' The blind man said to him, 'My teacher, let me see again.' Jesus said to him, 'Go; your faith has made you well.' Immediately he regained his sight and followed him on the way.

DO YOU REMEMBER THAT OLD JOKE ABOUT MRS THATCHER sitting down in a restaurant for a meal with the members of her cabinet?

'What will you have for your main course, Madam?' enquires the waiter.

'Beef!' replies Margaret decisively.

'Yes, Madam. And your vegetables?'

'Oh, they'll have the same as me.'

Now cast your mind back (patience – I'll get to the point in a minute) to the Tory party conference where sixteen-year-old William Hague, blessed with a strange little rustic hat of hair in those days, made that cocky speech about his intention of taking over Margaret Thatcher's job at some point in his political future. Immediately after he said this there was one eternal moment in which nobody moved or spoke. Then, breaking into the silence, came the sound of one person clapping – one highly significant person. It was Margaret Thatcher, the Prime Minister. As if fearful that they had missed a cue, the ministers on either side of her hastily plastered similarly indulgent smiles onto their faces and joined in the applause. They had clearly anticipated her shifting into disapproval mode, but they hardly missed a beat in making the U-turn.

That is exactly what seems to have happened in this encounter with Bartimaeus. Those who began by sternly telling the blind man off for making such a noise, switched to warm, coaxing encouragement as soon as Jesus showed an interest in the man's passionate expression of need. There is a long and rather dishonourable tradition of henchmen misrepresenting their masters or mistresses. In the Christian church it often manifests itself as a pessimistic belief that God is highly unlikely to give you what you want simply because you want it. Jesus wanted to heal Bartimaeus, so he did.

The truth is that there are certainly times when God lets us have what we want, even though we don't need it in any obvious way, and, perhaps rather more frequently, he gives us what we need, whether we want it or not. Jesus said that our heavenly Father knows what we need before we ask, but how does he manage to respond to us with such pin-point accuracy? Well, by knowing us so completely, of course.

Human beings, rather predictably, fall short of these high standards.

Take our friend Lily, for instance. I have written about Lily on a number of occasions because I think she is so lovely. She is an ex-missionary, well into her eighties and quite frail, but enormous fun, and a real old warrior for God. She goes to our church and is a member of the group that meets in our house each week.

Lily was once the proud possessor of a very distinctive pair of pyjamas, bought at a street-market in some distant land. Bright, light and lovely, these garments were made of thin cotton, very cool in hot weather, and decorated with a highly coloured Chinese pattern. They added a glow of joy to those nights when she wore them. However, all flesh is grass, and all pyjamas wear out. Eventually, Lily was reluctantly obliged to consign her favourite nightwear to the dustbin. Sad, but inevitable.

Then, one day, a friend mentioned that she would be in Singapore during the next couple of weeks.

'Ooh!' said Lily, suddenly inspired, 'if you're going to that part of the world, is there any chance you could get me a pair of pyjamas? You see, I really want a pair made of that thin cotton and decorated with colourful Chinese motifs – that sort of thing.'

The friend was happy to oblige. Returning a few weeks later, she handed Lily a parcel, insisting that she would take no money in return. Excitedly, Lily unwrapped her present, only to find a pair of thick woollen pyjamas decorated with little flowers, just right for an old lady, and no different from the pyjamas you can buy in any clothes shop in any High Street in any town in England.

Lily hid her disappointment. It had been very kind of the friend to take the trouble. Still, she had been looking forward to those pyjamas …

Her hopes were revived two or three weeks later on hearing that another friend was making a trip to Hong Kong. 'Made of that thin cotton,' pleaded Lily on the telephone, 'and decorated with lovely colourful Chinese motifs – if you wouldn't mind.'

The lady was happy to indulge her elderly friend.

'You don't have to give me any money, Lily,' she said on returning a fortnight later. It's a gift.'

'Oh, thank you!' said Lily excitedly, taking the paper from her gift to reveal a pair of thick woollen pyjamas decorated with a pale blue stripe, the sort of pyjamas, in fact, that you could buy in any shop in any High Street in any town in England.

You can see what had happened, can't you? These nice but blinkered people had been unable to genuinely accept the notion that an elderly lady of eighty-six could possibly *really* want thin cotton pyjamas with a highly-coloured Chinese motif, so they bought something that, as far as they were concerned, was more suitable. All very understandable – but so *annoying*. Why couldn't they have given Lily what she wanted?

I can tell you that we intend to buy Lily a pair of thin cotton pyjamas with a colourful Chinese motif as soon as possible!

By contrast, when Bridget and Kate and I were in Europe a few months ago, we found ourselves billeted for a few days in a sort of furnished outhouse on the edge of a river in somebody's back garden, and felt quite disgruntled at first. It was freezing cold, and – dare I admit this further cause for complaint? – there was no television! Why had we landed in this place? The answer soon became apparent. Our hosts had three little girls and one boy who adopted Kate from the first moment they saw her. Suddenly, instead of being a sort of adjunct to her touring parents, she was a star in the universe of these energetic little children who adored her. It was *such* a good thing to happen at that stage of our trip. Additionally, there were very necessary and significant conversations to be held between Bridget and the mother of these children, the details of which need not be mentioned here.

What a relief it is that God knows each of us so much better than Lily's friends know her. He has noted the desire of our hearts, and whenever possible he will grant it. And how reassuring that sometimes, as with our experience in chilly central Europe, he gives us what we need and allows us to discover that, in the light of events, it just happens to also be exactly what we want.

58

Jesus' Triumphal Entry into Jerusalem

11 : 1 – 11

When they were approaching Jerusalem, at Bethphage and Bethany, near the Mount of Olives, he sent two of his disciples and said to them, 'Go into the village ahead of you, and immediately as you enter it, you will find tied there a colt that has never been ridden; untie it and bring it. If anyone says to you, "Why are you doing this?" just say this, "The Lord needs it and will send it back here immediately." '

They went away and found a colt tied near a door, outside in the street. As they were untying it, some of the bystanders said to them, 'What are you doing, untying the colt?' They told them what Jesus had said; and they allowed them to take it.

Then they brought the colt to Jesus and threw their cloaks on it; and he sat on it. Many people spread their cloaks on the road, and others spread leafy branches that they had cut in the fields. Then those who went ahead and those who followed were shouting, 'Hosanna! Blessed is the one who comes in the name of the Lord! Blessed is the coming kingdom of our ancestor David! Hosanna in the highest heaven!'

Then he entered Jerusalem and went into the temple; and when he had looked around at everything, as it was already late, he went out to Bethany with the twelve.

As some of you may be aware, I have never ceased to be fascinated by the idea of the two disciples in the first part of this passage setting off to perform what, on the face of it, seems a fairly simple task. Would you not agree, though, that quite a high percentage of fairly simple looking tasks turn out to be much more tricky in practice than in theory? That is as true now as it must have been two thousand years ago. I don't wish to be uncharitable towards these two heroes of the New Testament, but I can't help feeling that it could have been a little bit like this:

A: *(Uneasily, as they arrive in the middle of the town and spot a colt)* Well, do you think this is it – or not?

B: I dunno! I don't know any more than you, do I? I – I mean, it's a colt.

A: Yes, thank you, I know it's a colt. What I mean is – is it *the* colt? Does it look as if it's been ridden?

B: *(Irritably)* Does it look as if it's been ridden? How am I supposed to know if it's been ridden just by looking at it? Did you think there'd be a bit of a dent in the middle? Why don't you ask it? You and it probably speak the same language.

A: That's not funny, you know. That's silly. *(Thinks)* Tell you what – just get on it and see if it throws you off.

B: What!

A: Then if it throws you off we'll know it hasn't been ridden.

B: *(Patiently, as to an imbecile)* But it will have been ridden, won't it? By me.

A: Yes, but only for a split second, and that won't matter because it's whether it had been ridden before you got on that counts, so -

B: Sorry – sorry, can I just stop you there? It's a really great plan. One little tiny adjustment. Why don't *you* just get on it and see if it throws *you* off.

A: *(Sternly)* Look, don't you want to obey the Lord's command?

B: No. Yes. Don't you?

A: Yes, but – oh, well, look it's probably all right, there are no other colts in sight, are there? This must be the right one. Go on – untie it.

B: Me? *Me?* I'm not untying it. You're the clever one with all the ideas. You untie it. I'm not untying it. *(Sigh)* I wish I'd never come now. Anyway, I seem to remember someone telling me that it's wrong to dabble in a colt.

A: In the occult I think you'll find that is.

B: Oh, is it? Oh, right.

A: Oh, dear, we're not getting very far, are we?! *(Pause)* Look, how about if we just go back and tell him we had a good look round, but we didn't see any colts?

A & B: *(After a moment's thought)* No-o-o-o ...

A: Come on – you untie it.

B: No, you untie it.

A: No, you!

B: No you!

A: You!

B: You!

A: No, y – oh, all right, come here, I'll do it.

B: Aah! It's the owners! They want to know what we're doing with their colt!

A: Oh, blimey! What was it he said? What did he say we had to say?

B: Tell 'em the Lord needs it. Go on, say it! *(Covers face)*

A: *(High-pitched)* Err, the Lord hath need of it.

B: Have they gone?

A: Yes, they've gone, oh, mighty spiritual warrior. You can come out now.

B: Ooh, thank goodness for that!

A: Come on, grab this rope – let's get out of here.

B: I wish it had been a fish. You know where you are with fish. A fish that's never been – ridden. Would've spotted it a mile off. I *know* fish ...

Whatever complications there may have been, these two did return with a colt, and it was on this animal that Jesus enjoyed the only wholehearted public worship of his three year ministry. A sublime moment, but was this the same crowd who would later scream for him to be crucified?

59

Jesus Curses the Fig Tree and Cleanses the Temple

11 : 12 – 19

On the following day, when they came from Bethany, he was hungry. Seeing in the distance a fig tree in leaf, he went to see whether perhaps he would find anything on it. When he came to it, he found nothing but leaves, for it was not the season for figs. He said to it, 'May no one ever eat fruit from you again.' And his disciples heard it.

Then they came to Jerusalem. And he entered the temple and began to drive out those who were selling and those who were buying in the temple, and he overturned the tables of the money changers and the seats of those who sold doves; and he would not allow anyone to carry anything through the temple.

He was teaching and saying, 'Is it not written, "My house shall be called a house of prayer for all the nations"? But you have made it a den of robbers.'

And when the chief priests and the scribes heard it, they kept looking for a way to kill him; for they were afraid of him, because the whole crowd was spellbound by his teaching. And when evening came, Jesus and his disciples went out of the city.

E ARLIER ON IN THIS BOOK I REVEALED THAT, INCREDIBLY, A joint committee of twenty-first century Christian organisations and church leaders were given the opportunity to report on Jesus' plans for ministry and parables before he actually arrived on earth. We have seen what they thought of his parables. Here is an edited summary of their comments on his life and ministry.

We now turn to the ideas that you have put forward concerning those items of your life and ministry that should be recorded for posterity. None of us is in any doubt that you have worked very hard in compiling your list of things to do, but, as with the parables, we would counsel you against inconsistency and a tendency to over-dramatise yourself. If what you have to say and do is worth saying and doing then there is no need to embroider or embellish it. You must also constantly bear in mind your theoretically sinless state. Either you are without sin, or you are not. There can be no grey areas.

Some specific points.

Have you thought seriously about the implications of your 'born in a stable' scenario? Do you not feel that the God who created the earth, who brought the Israelites out of bondage, who sends an angel to speak to your mother and father, and who summons wise men and shepherds (are the shepherds absolutely necessary?) to the place of your birth, is more than capable of arranging reasonable accommodation for the birth of his son? You are planning a life, young man, not writing a Russian novel, and God must be honoured in all things.

We can only think that you were suffering some kind of brainstorm when you postulated the murder of hundreds of innocent children by Herod. The very idea of your life and safety being bought at such a hideous cost is one that no right-thinking person could even contemplate. A morbid streak? Something for you to consider, perhaps.

We come now to your suggestion that, at the age of twelve, you should deviously escape the care of your father and mother for three days at the festival of Passover, and be found eventually by them having deep discussions in the temple. A lady member of our committee who has successfully raised three sons and one daughter was absolutely aghast, as indeed we all were, at the notion that children of a similar age reading this account should be led to assume that deserting their parents for days without a word of explanation or warning is a perfectly acceptable way of behaving. The pain and worry and fear caused by such behaviour can only be understood by those who have actually experienced it. Sinless? We think not. Virtue must not be sacrificed at the altar of dramatic force.

On that subject, one of our longest standing members, a lifelong teetotaller, suggests that you might like to reconsider details of the water into wine incident. Is there a cogent reason, he asks, why the water in question should not be turned into non-alcoholic wine or blackcurrant cordial, or at the very least, rather unpleasant, vinegary wine? Leading others into sin by tempting them with the best wine at the end of a celebration is really not very helpful to the weaker brother.

Now, in our comments on the parables we did make a plea for you to remember that the things you say and do are *not* intended for one era only. In this connection we really do feel that the incident in which you plan to curse a fig tree is gravely ill-advised. Your motives may be excellent, but what appears to be a petulant outburst and a wanton act of destruction on your part simply because you cannot have any figs, will not go down at all well with members of the Green Party, a movement that is quite active in our age. It is a matter of sensitivity. You may make your point, but you will lose the respect and interest of people who love God's created world. Worth it?

Finally, we must make mention of your extraordinary plan to, as you put it, 'cleanse' the temple. In other sections of this report we have made quite clear our total opposition to the shrapnel-bursts of abuse and criticism with which you plan to 'rake' some of the most respectable and influential members of the society into which you will be born. You know, you cannot preach about turning the other cheek, and then ridicule and insult those who are against you. There is a word for that. The word is 'hypocrisy', and *it does not win converts*. The basic problem with this temple cleansing business is exactly the same in essence. You simply cannot walk around preaching love, peace, and joy, and then, in the next instant, start throwing tables around and beating people violently with knotted ropes just because they are doing something that you do not happen to like or approve of.

You seem, if you do not mind us making this point, extremely confused as to the real nature of sin. You cannot simply select items of behaviour and assert that, because you have performed them, they are in some way acceptable. The reverse should be the case for all of us. We must accept a blue-print for behaviour, such as the ten commandments, and then we must make a moral assessment of the things we do or plan to do within that context. If there is another way to approach these matters – well, we as a committee would love to hear what it could possibly be.

Your project is a very important and commendable one, and we would not wish to discourage you. For it to have any real hope of success, however, you must look seriously at the areas we have mentioned. The two C's, Consistency and Compromise will be your best guides. We look forward to receiving your revised plans.

Yours etc.

60

The Lesson from the Withered Fig Tree

11 : 20 – 25

In the morning as they passed by, they saw the fig tree withered away to its roots. Then Peter remembered and said to him, 'Rabbi, look! The fig tree that you cursed has withered.'

Jesus answered them, 'Have faith in God. Truly I tell you, if you say to this mountain, "Be taken up and thrown into the sea," and if you do not doubt in your heart, but believe that what you say will come to pass, it will be done for you. So I tell you, whatever you ask for in prayer, believe that you have received it, and it will be yours. Whenever you stand praying, forgive, if you have any-thing against anyone; so that your Father in heaven may also for-give you your trespasses.'

M OST OF US, AT ONE TIME OR ANOTHER, HAVE REACHED A point where we wonder why the thing that we call our 'Christian life' doesn't seem to be moving forward at all. Leaving aside the difficulty of knowing precisely what that question means, it is worth considering whether we have taken on board some of these very basic teachings of Jesus.

Incidentally, the more alert among you may have noticed that this passage ends at verse twenty-five, while the following passage begins with verse twenty-seven. The missing section, one of those iffy verses that some translators leave in and some leave out, states quite bluntly that if we do not forgive our enemies God will not forgive us. In the sixth chapter of Matthew's gospel you will find a non-iffy verse that says exactly the same thing. It is, in any case, implied by verse twenty-five, and more familiarly, by that part of the Lord's Prayer which asks the Father to forgive our trespasses as we forgive the trespasses of others.

Whatever the validity of that extra verse, and however you want to look at the issue, Jesus is clearly very serious about the need for us to take an attitude of forgiveness before we start asking anything for ourselves, whether it's shifting the odd mountain or repenting of our impatience with ancient Auntie Alice.

'But what if I simply *can't* forgive? What if I really, really try to forgive this person I hate but I just can't do it?'

I suspect that the answer to this question is exactly the same as the answer to many similar ones. Two principles are very valuable in guiding us – honesty and obedience. At Gethsemane Jesus opened up his terror to his Father, asking for the cup to be taken from him, but committing himself to obedience if that was not possible. Being honest with God, telling him that we see the need to forgive, but that we can't actually feel it at all, is perfectly right and proper. The next step is, as a matter of obedience, to pray for the person concerned – through gritted teeth if necessary. God has always honoured that combination of truthfulness and a determination to do what one is told.

We must forgive if we are to be forgiven. There is no way around that fact.

Some crimes are so horrendous that it is difficult to see how forgiveness can ever enter into the equation. Do you remember the intense discussion a few years ago about a court decision involving the killers of Jamie Bulger. Eight years previously two-year-old Jamie had been lured from a railway station and callously murdered by two boys aged ten and eleven. These boys had been in secure custody since the incident, but now, at the age of eighteen, release was imminent and future plans had to be made.

The decision I have just referred to concerned the right of these convicted killers to be relocated and furnished with new identities to protect them from acts of violence that might be committed by those who had threatened to avenge Jamie's death. The announcement that the two offenders would indeed be protected in this way was greeted with passionate outrage by a majority of the public. Protesters pointed out that the parents of the murdered boy were enduring a life sentence of grief and pain. Why, they asked, should Jamie's killers serve only eight years before being given everything they needed to lead a free and anonymous life?

I understood this response. I was a long way from understanding it fully, of course, because I had not lost my child in such unspeakable circumstances. I had children, though, and I did have occasional nightmares. So far, thank God, I had always woken up from them.

The contribution to the debate that I did feel qualified to make sprung from memories of time spent in contact with teenage offenders earlier in my life. The secure assessment unit in which I worked was near Birmingham, and was used as a facility for teenagers who could not be placed in open units. These might include violent children, absconders, or those who, like Jamie Bulger's killers, had committed crimes so serious that they needed to be held in a secure situation until their case came to trial.

Reaction to such incidents as the Bulger murder very often features a question about how anyone could possibly look one of those boys in the eye and see anything but a monster.

So, what happens when you actually meet one of these 'monsters'?

One day the staff in our unit received a message that a new boy was on his way. He would arrive in one hour, and we must be ready to deal with him when he was brought in by the police.

The reasons for admission made appalling reading. This boy and his friend had knocked on the door of a lady who was in her eighties. They pretended to be lads who sometimes helped the pensioner with her shopping. Having been allowed in they attacked her, injuring her head so badly that she fell bleeding and unconscious onto the kitchen floor. The two boys then escaped with thirty pounds that they found upstairs. Their elderly victim lay insensible for forty-eight hours. By the time someone did get worried enough to force entry she was dead.

We cleared the decks to receive this particular monster. Anything breakable was stowed away. The other six residents of the unit were locked in their rooms. Three of us waited, almost half-crouching at the top of the stairs like slip-fielders in a game of cricket, ready to subdue this wild boy. We had already said how much we loathed him without even meeting him. There was a general, muttered consensus that if ever anyone deserved to be given a hard time and no sympathy at all, it was this vicious young thug. At last, we heard the sound of double locks clattering and turning at the bottom of the stairs, and, seconds later, the killer stood before us.

The monster was so small. And so terrified. And so confused. And so unmonster-like.

As I went through the normal admission procedures I really did try to rekindle the negative attitudes that had burned in my heart on learning what he had done, and as I had waited for him at the top of the stairs. I couldn't do it. Whether I should have been able to do it or not, I just couldn't. I certainly wasn't soft with him. But neither was I deliberately vindictive or cold.

He was a very frightened little boy, and I could feel only compassion.

None of this is to do with condoning awful crimes. I certainly don't. And if you ask me how I would have felt if he had murdered my mother or daughter, the answer is that I would probably have wanted to do something horribly violent to him in return. No, for me, as a Christian, it is simply yet another reminder that I am pinning all my hopes on Jesus greeting me at the gates of heaven, not with the harsh words and punishment that my wrong-doing deserves, but with a warm and miraculous compassion for the frightened child inside me.

In the meantime, I am commanded to do the same for others.

Did you know, by the way, that 'forgiveness' is an anagram of 'serving foes'?

61

Jesus' Authority
Is Questioned

11 : 27 – 33

Again they came to Jerusalem. As he was walking in the temple, the chief priests, the scribes, and the elders came to him and said, 'By what authority are you doing these things? Who gave you this authority to do them?'

Jesus said to them, 'I will ask you one question; answer me, and I will tell you by what authority I do these things. Did the baptism of John come from heaven, or was it of human origin? Answer me.'

They argued with one another, 'If we say, "From heaven," he will say, "Why then did you not believe him?" But shall we say, "Of human origin"?' — they were afraid of the crowd, for all regarded John as truly a prophet. So they answered Jesus, 'We do not know.'

And Jesus said to them, 'Neither will I tell you by what authority I am doing these things.'

A FTER A FEW MINUTES OF HUDDLED, WHISPERING, HISSED
confabulation, the reply that eventually emerged from this
group of high-powered individuals must have seemed a risible
anti-climax to onlookers, mustn't it?

Picture it.

Jesus asks his question – worried pause – turn away – mutter, mutter, mutter – turn back again – all try to be the one
standing at the back – one gets pushed to the front – clearing
of the throat – dramatic pause:

'Err, we don't know ...'

Ribald laughter from the crowd.

I wonder if that unfortunate spokesman made an effort to
invest those three words with the dignity normally associated
with such exalted persons. Did he narrow his eyes, stroke his
beard, and pronounce them in a meditative, reflective sort of
way, as though there were many excellent replies available and
it was merely a matter of selecting the most appropriate? Even
if he did, I don't suppose anyone was very impressed. Foiled
again!

Here is yet another example of what I have described elsewhere as the metaphorical ju-jitsu which Jesus employed with
such skill against those who attacked him. Over the shoulder of
the Son of God go those very important pillars of society, pro-
pelled by the momentum of their own fear and prejudice, landing with a painful thump precisely on the spot where he
intended them to be.

I can tell you from experience that this process still happens
today. If we are asinine enough to take God on with consciously
ill-motivated questions (and believe me, plenty of us do), he will
probably ask us a highly significant question in return. Before
we know it we shall be flying through the air and praying for a
soft landing.

62

The Parable of
the Wicked Tenants

12 : 1 – 12

Then he began to speak to them in parables.

'A man planted a vineyard, put a fence around it, dug a pit for the wine press, and built a watchtower; then he leased it to tenants and went to another country. When the season came, he sent a slave to the tenants to collect from them his share of the produce of the vineyard. But they seized him, and beat him, and sent him away empty-handed. And again he sent another slave to them; this one they beat over the head and insulted. Then he sent another, and that one they killed. And so it was with many others; some they beat, and others they killed. He had still one other, a beloved son. Finally he sent him to them, saying, "They will respect my son."

'But those tenants said to one another, "This is the heir; come, let us kill him, and the inheritance will be ours."

'So they seized him, killed him, and threw him out of the vineyard. What then will the owner of the vineyard do? He will come and destroy the tenants and give the vineyard to others. Have you not read this scripture:

"The stone that the builders rejected has become the cornerstone; this was the Lord's doing, and it is amazing in our eyes"?'

When they realized that he had told this parable against them, they wanted to arrest him, but they feared the crowd. So they left him and went away.

HOW COULD RECORD COMPANIES HAVE FAILED TO SEE THE talent and potential of The Beatles in the days before they became famous? They must have wept and gnashed their teeth and kicked their own corporate bottoms afterwards. How could so many publishers have remained blind to the immense talent and writing skills of James Herriot in the days before just about everyone seemed to become entranced by descriptions of a country vet sticking his arm up a cow's backside? Moving rapidly from the sublime to the ridiculous, when I first began writing I had many early manuscripts rejected by Christian publishers. Attached to one of these was a little note explaining that the publisher concerned felt that his readers would 'not wish the Lord Jesus Christ to be portrayed in this manner'. Mind you, some may still agree with that comment. An awful lot don't.

Here, then, at the beginning of the twelfth chapter of Mark's gospel, Jesus uses the parable of the tenants to highlight the worst example of this phenomenon of unrecognised excellence that one can possibly imagine. The Messiah, son of the creator God, was about to be aggressively rejected by people whose eternal lives depended on him. They were blind to who he was and where he had come from, ignorant of the fact that whatever religious edifice they built in the future was bound to fall because its essential foundation stone was missing.

Every now and then I am overcome by feelings of desolation when I think that, in this age, exactly the same thing is happening, especially in countries such as ours. Partly because we have so misrepresented our faith in the past, and partly because the material world has become so deeply distracting, Jesus is rejected out of hand, often by people who have only the haziest notion of who he is and what he is about. I'm afraid it's up to us, folks, with the guidance and wisdom of God, and through the power of his Spirit, to wake our communities to the reality of their own need, and to the central part that Jesus is willing to play in their lives.

63

The Question about Paying Taxes

12 : 13 – 17

Then they sent to him some Pharisees and some Herodians to trap him in what he said. And they came and said to him, 'Teacher, we know that you are sincere, and show deference to no one; for you do not regard people with partiality, but teach the way of God in accordance with truth. Is it lawful to pay taxes to the emperor, or not? Should we pay them, or should we not?'

But knowing their hypocrisy, he said to them, 'Why are you putting me to the test? Bring me a denarius and let me see it.'

And they brought one.

Then he said to them, 'Whose head is this, and whose title?'

They answered, 'The emperor's.'

Jesus said to them, 'Give to the emperor the things that are the emperor's, and to God the things that are God's.'

And they were utterly amazed at him.

THERE ARE TWO PEOPLE I GREATLY ADMIRE, WHOSE COMMENTS on this passage are not in agreement with my own. One is Dennis Potter, distinguished English television playwright, the other is Richard Wurmbrandt, Romanian pastor, and author of 'Tortured for Christ', his celebrated account of a fourteen-year ordeal at the hands of the secret police in his home country. In one way it is fortunate for me that these men are no longer with us. They were both cleverer than I am and would certainly have demolished any argument I put forward within seconds. Now, of course, both of them are in possession of the absolute truth, so, who knows? Perhaps they are itching to tell me that they were wrong and I am right. Well, perhaps not ...

Potter wrote a play about Jesus way back in the sixties that was simply called 'Son of Man'. In it the Messiah appears as a not particularly likeable little man with an unpleasant manner and a rather grubby persona. Like nearly all of Dennis Potter's work it was an entertaining and stimulating piece of television, but I hated the Jesus that it portrayed. One line sticks in my memory. The Pharisees and Herodians put the question about paying taxes to Jesus, he asks them to produce a denarius and when they do so he asks whose head appears on the coin. They reply that it is Caesar's head, and, as far as I can remember, Jesus then says the following:

'Give God what is God's, and Caesar what is Caesar's – and shut up!'

I know Jesus gave these fellows a very hard time, but I simply do not believe that he was scoring off them for the sake of it, nor that he was capable of sounding so cheap and nasty.

Wurmbrandt's interpretation of Jesus' remark is completely different, and may have sprung from long experience of living under an oppressive regime. His contention was that when Jesus told them to give Caesar what was due to Caesar he was actually saying that the Jews should boot the Roman invaders out of their country. I don't go for that either, piquant though the idea is. Jesus was never political in the narrow sense, in fact he seemed reluctant to align himself with any movement at all other than the spiritual and historical fulfilment of scripture.

No, I believe that, apart from dealing successfully with yet another trick question from the Pharisees, Jesus was also making the serious point that respect for temporal authority and obedience to God are both required from believers, and that they are not necessarily mutually exclusive.

So! As Jesus himself so often asked – what do *you* think?

64

The Question about the Resurrection

12 : 18 – 27

Some Sadducees, who say there is no resurrection, came to him and asked him a question, saying, 'Teacher, Moses wrote for us that "if a man's brother dies, leaving a wife but no child, the man shall marry the widow and raise up children for his brother." There were seven brothers; the first married and, when he died, left no children; and the second married her and died, leaving no children; and the third likewise; none of the seven left children. Last of all the woman herself died. In the resurrection whose wife will she be? For the seven had married her.'

Jesus said to them, 'Is not this the reason you are wrong, that you know neither the scriptures nor the power of God? For when they rise from the dead, they neither marry nor are given in marriage, but are like angels in heaven. And as for the dead being raised, have you not read in the book of Moses, in the story about the bush, how God said to him, "I am the God of Abraham, the God of Isaac, and the God of Jacob"? He is God not of the dead, but of the living; you are quite wrong.'

THESE SAD SADDUCEES! HOW DISAPPOINTED THEY MUST have been when their intricately devised question was disposed of with such vigour and optimism. However, I have a sneaking suspicion that I produce equally silly queries sometimes. C. S. Lewis once pointed out that many of the questions we address to God are not really questions at all because they arise from a profound poverty of wisdom and understanding. It is, for instance, he says, as though we were asking to be told the shape of yellow.

The sheer, ebullient confidence of Jesus when he speaks about the certainty of resurrection has drawn me out of darkness again and again. I have been subject to occasional fits of morbid dread throughout my life, and although I recognise the root and the unreliability of such feelings, they can mar the happiest of times

One particular summer's day comes to mind because it was *such* a happy day. It was a family outing. Bridget drove the car and I sat in the front passenger seat. Behind sat my father-in-law, who was ninety-four, his wife Kathleen, a toddler of eighty-six, and their old friend Kath who was staying for a few days. Kath, nearly ninety, was struggling to decide whether or not to emigrate to Australia to be near her children and grandchildren for the remaining years of her life.

Our little expedition was a happy one. For once, the world was not just sunny and domed with blue, it was enjoying what the British call a 'glorious day'. Too glorious, perhaps, with temperatures up above the thirty mark, but the air-conditioning in our car was deliciously efficient. Watching the heat from a cool interior is almost as satisfying as watching rain from under cover.

Then there was the countryside we were driving through. If you are familiar with the bottom right-hand corner of England you will know the green, gently undulating charm of the richly-foliaged counties of Kent and Sussex. Gardens were bursting, birds were auditioning away like mad, and, here and there, shirtless, shorted men in wide-brimmed hats happily, lazily prodded the earth in the front gardens of their cottages.

Our destination, a public garden called Merriments, close to the village of Hurst Green, revealed itself as exquisite. Bank upon bank of gorgeously coloured flowers surrounded a small lake whose mill-pond stillness was nearly covered with water-lily pads. Oohing and aahing over the more spectacular blooms, we explored the network of grassy walkways winding between beautifully maintained beds, and finally made our way to the restaurant connected to the establishment, where we ate a pleasant, light lunch in the open air. After lunch Bridget and her mother bought a plant or two to take back for their own gardens.

Shortly after leaving we stopped the car to buy two pounds of sweet, ripe cherries from a stall at the side of the road (good cherries are about as near to ambrosia as we are likely to experience here on earth), then made a detour towards the south, picking up the coast road so that as much of our return journey as possible could be within sight of the ocean. Bowling along between the Eastbourne to Hastings railway line on our right and Cooden Beach on our left we hugged the line of the shore for miles, eating the cherries we had been going to save for tea, and watching the waveless expanse of aquamarine water dance with a billion points of light in the late afternoon sunshine.

Indulgently, we allowed ourselves to be seduced by the idea of taking afternoon tea at the Hydro Hotel in Eastbourne, just to finish off the day. What a place! Perched high above the western end of Eastbourne, the Hydro Hotel has for many years been an island of old-fashioned Englishness, the ideal setting for an Agatha Christie mystery, and one of the last places on earth where they really do understand what a Sussex Cream Tea should look like. After tea we wandered out onto the lawn, stretching out towards the distant ocean like the prow of a green ship, to sit and watch a group of hotel residents playing a leisurely game of croquet on the grassy deck. Let me tell you – it really does not get much more English than that.

Many things to enjoy. Many reasons to be happy. And I promise you that I do not work for the East Sussex Tourist Board. They are all true. I enjoyed them and I was happy. So why, I asked myself, as I got ready for bed that night, had there been that unmistakable shadow of sadness upon me throughout a very happy day? I think it was something to do with the growing awareness Bridget and I had of the age and frailty of her parents, particularly her father, who could walk only very short distances by then. Added to this was Kath's dilemma. While she was fit, living in England would not be a problem, but what would happen if – or when – she became ill and helpless. By the time that day was upon her, it would be too late for the big decision ...

I was probably sad for every one of us stumbling pilgrims. On a day in which we had seen such beautiful things there seemed to be an added poignancy about the inevitability of leaving a world that can be as sweet and fragrant as it is sometimes harsh. Whether it is on the slopes of Gethsemane or in the garden of the Hydro Hotel, none of us are able to escape that moment when we look around at the world we belong to and the faces of those whom we love, and feel our hearts failing us at the prospect of such profound and apparently unavoidable loss.

I do sincerely thank the God of the Living that Jesus was able to speak with such excitement and boldness about the resurrection of the dead, and that he has so triumphantly overcome death.

65

The First Commandment

12 : 28 – 34

One of the scribes came near and heard them disputing with one another, and seeing that he answered them well, he asked him, 'Which commandment is the first of all?'

Jesus answered, 'The first is, "Hear, O Israel: the Lord our God, the Lord is one; you shall love the Lord your God with all your heart, and with all your soul, and with all your mind, and with all your strength." The second is this, "You shall love your neighbour as yourself." There is no other commandment greater than these.'

Then the scribe said to him, 'You are right, Teacher; you have truly said that "he is one, and besides him there is no other"; and "to love him with all the heart, and with all the understanding, and with all the strength," and "'to love one's neighbour as oneself," – this is much more important than all whole burnt offerings and sacrifices.'

When Jesus saw that he answered wisely, he said to him, 'You are not far from the kingdom of God.'

After that no one dared to ask him any question.

THIS IS ONE OF THE GREAT SIGNPOST PASSAGES IN THE NEW Testament, isn't it? All through the Old Testament there is a continual if sometimes veiled revelation of the fact that the outward forms of religious observance are more to do with the needs of man than of Jehovah. Love, justice, truth and care for others are the true priorities of the creator who once enjoyed walking with Adam in the cool of the afternoon. The rest, the burnt offerings and sacrifices and all the rest of it, were nothing more than a means to an end, visual aids for a people who, at their worst, were unable to believe in or respond to anything that they could not actually see and touch. And here is Jesus confirming that truth, allowing the sanity of God to break into the foolishness of men, making it quite clear that all the negative commands and symbolic practices in past present or future are eternally contained in and consumed by two magnificently positive commandments. Love God with everything that you are and have, and serve your neighbour as though you are loving and serving yourself. In other words, let the law be written on your hearts, rather than on tablets of stone.

I have often wondered if this scribe was flattered to hear that he was not far from the kingdom of God? I suspect that he was. Bright-eyed and bushy-tailed, no doubt. And do you not think that he might have found Jesus later and asked him, 'Er, teacher, you know you said I was not far from the kingdom of God. Well, what do I have to do to actually – you know – get there? What is the final step?'

Ah! There is the vital question for us all.

The Question
about David's Son

12 : 35 – 37
While Jesus was teaching in the temple, he said, 'How can the
scribes say that the Messiah is the son of David? David himself, by
the Holy Spirit, declared, "The Lord said to my Lord, 'Sit at my
right hand, until I put your enemies under your feet.' " David himself calls him Lord; so how can he be his son?' And the large
crowd was listening to him with delight.

T HE LITERARY STYLE OF THE GOSPELS CAN, ON A SUPERFICIAL
reading, give a very solemn, po-faced view of the events
recorded therein. Here, though, a little window is opened for us
onto the sparkling style of delivery that Jesus often favoured,
and the way in which it was received by those who heard him.
He must have hugely enjoyed this particular occasion, and
clearly the large crowd loved it. They were as delighted (precisely the right word) with his theological plate-spinning as you
or I are when we hear or read ideas that wake our hearts and
minds up with their freshness and logical athleticism. Old arguments dusted down and rearranged by an expert can be utterly
captivating. Almost *edible*. Jesus was a master of the art.

Speaking of being po-faced, I well remember my first trips
to Germany as a speaker. In those very early days a significant
proportion of the audience – perhaps they saw themselves as a
congregation – would enter the hall or church as though they
were attending the funeral of a friend or close family member.
Presumably they felt that a 'religious' occasion necessitated a
demeanour of sobriety and grave concentration. This rarely

lasted for very long. As soon as permission to laugh or cry or think or ask questions was granted the sun would come out and the dark clouds of pseudo-reverence would be dispelled. Nowadays, thank God, people are already smiling when they come in.

The large crowd mentioned in this passage learned two things. They learned, if they were listening properly, that the Messiah was proclaiming a spiritual kingdom as opposed to a temporal one, and that the Son of God was an engaging and entertaining speaker. Not bad for one day, was it?

67

Jesus Denounces the Scribes

12 : 38 – 40

As he taught, he said, 'Beware of the scribes, who like to walk around in long robes, and to be greeted with respect in the marketplaces, and to have the best seats in the synagogues and places of honour at banquets! They devour widows' houses and for the sake of appearance say long prayers. They will receive the greater condemnation.'

THERE WE ARE, THEN. A RATHER SIMPLE MESSAGE HERE. IF you or I are strutting around being wonderfully spiritual on the outside and not giving a tinker's elbow for anyone on the inside, we're going to get it in the neck. Is that clear enough? It is for me. We had better pray for ourselves and others.

The Widow's Offering

12 : 41 – 44

He sat down opposite the treasury, and watched the crowd putting money into the treasury. Many rich people put in large sums. A poor widow came and put in two small copper coins, which are worth a penny. Then he called his disciples and said to them, 'Truly I tell you, this poor widow has put in more than all those who are contributing to the treasury. For all of them have contributed out of their abundance; but she out of her poverty has put in everything she had, all she had to live on.'

THIS LITTLE SNAPSHOT OF A MOMENT HAS SPOKEN FOR itself for two thousand years. It is worth bearing in mind, though, that in a different time and a different place it might just as easily have been called 'The Sad Man's Smile' or 'The Exhausted Woman's Effort' or 'The Impatient Man's Restraint' or 'The Selfish Woman's Kindness'.

I shall never forget one evening about fifteen years ago when I was sitting at home wrestling with some deeply depressing news that had arrived in the morning of that same day. The doorbell rang, and when I opened the door there stood a friend of mine with four cans of beer clutched in his hand. Having heard about my bad news he had decided to visit me, calling in at the off-licence on the way. It would have been a good idea and a friendly thing to do under any circumstances. What made it so particularly touching was that this chap, bless his soul, was, for reasons that do not concern us here, one of the meanest individuals I have ever known. The spending of every pound and every penny that he owned was, for him, a matter of grave, painful consideration. For this man to go into a shop and buy something that he didn't actually *have* to buy for the sake of making someone else a little happier, was really quite remarkable. I felt genuinely honoured that he had used up his entire stock of generosity on me.

Whatever it is that we don't have much of, if we give it all, we have given much. God will know.

The Destruction
of the Temple Foretold

13 : 1 – 8

As he came out of the temple, one of his disciples said to him, 'Look, Teacher, what large stones and what large buildings!' Then Jesus asked him, 'Do you see these great buildings? Not one stone will be left here upon another; all will be thrown down.' When he was sitting on the Mount of Olives opposite the temple, Peter, James, John, and Andrew asked him privately, 'Tell us, when will this be, and what will be the sign that all these things are about to be accomplished?' Then Jesus began to say to them, 'Beware that no one leads you astray. Many will come in my name and say, "I am he!" and they will lead many astray. When you hear of wars and rumours of wars, do not be alarmed; this must take place, but the end is still to come. For nation will rise against nation, and kingdom against kingdom; there will be earthquakes in various places; there will be famines. This is but the beginning of the birth pangs.'

PEOPLE SOMETIMES SAY THAT WE CHRISTIANS SHOULD believe everything we're told because we are supposed to be like sheep, and sheep are gullible. But sheep are not that gullible. They can be rather stupidly uniform in their behaviour, but they don't, for instance, eat stones or bits of wood. They eat grass. They don't go on expensive package holidays believing every unlikely word that some profit-motivated travel firm tells them. What they are good at is following people whom they trust. As Jesus says here, we have to be careful who we listen to and what we believe.

Several years ago I did a series of talks in Sweden. This short tour was organised by the firm that publishes my books in that country, and it began at a big music festival in Helsinki. I was ushered on to the stage of a vast arena to fill an echoing gap between the departure of one very heavy rock band and the arrival of another. The idea was that I would read an extract from 'The Sacred Diary' – in English – to thousands of Swedish teenage music fans who had never heard of me. So highly amused and entertained would this audience be, that they would hardly be able to restrain themselves from instantly rushing out and buying copies of my book. You will not be surprised to hear that this Baldrick-like cunning plan fell short of producing the required result. I suppose a tiny percentage of young people might actually have noticed me bleating away unhappily against the constant chatter and incessant plinking and plunking of musicians making their final check that they were definitely out of tune, but the only rational response was puzzlement. Why on earth was this strange foreigner bothering to mouth obscure things to an audience that was unable to hear or understand a word he was saying?

When I stepped down from the stage that evening I was in a state of shock. They talk about performers dying. I was in an advanced stage of rigor-mortis. And I was furious with myself. How could I have allowed my publishers to persuade me that getting up in front of all those people was a good idea? They explained afterwards that the very fact of my having partici-pated in the festival was helpful to them in publicising the book. That may or may not have been so. All I know is that I felt a complete fool for being mad enough to go along with their plans.

The rest of the tour was completely different, thank goodness.

Another experience like that might have put me off public speaking for ever. I did, however, learn another lesson in Sweden about the dangers of too easily accepting what others say. This time it was not me who was gullible, but a whole church full of Christians.

I have mentioned elsewhere the tendency of Christian groups to sit like rows of baby birds, waiting for truths and teaching to be dropped into their wide-open beaks by whoever is the spiritual 'parent' of the moment. Never have I seen this more graphically illustrated than at the extremely charismatic church which I spoke at halfway through my Swedish tour.

Walking in through the doors of the church I had noticed a girl with a pet monkey on her shoulder. Speakers are always looking for something on which to hang their opening remarks. The monkey would do very nicely. Hopefully it would give everybody a laugh right at the beginning of my talk. I kept my face very straight as, with an interpreter's assistance, I started to speak in that sonorous, divinely intimate, close-to-the-microphone voice so beloved of Christian speakers almost everywhere.

'I just want to say that I noticed a girl over there with a monkey on her shoulder. I feel the Lord is telling me he would have us all equipped with monkeys. I believe that the people of this church are about to receive the Gift of Monkeys.'

I waited for someone to laugh at this absurd notion. Nobody did. I looked along the rows of faces. Some of them were expressing slight surprise, but only some of them, and it was only slight. I had an uneasy feeling that, by Sunday week at the earliest, every person in this church would have a monkey on his or her shoulder. This church would become famous in Sweden for having started the new 'Monkey Wave', then it would spread across the entire world and it would be my fault.

I was about to feebly explain that I had been joking, when there was the faintest of nervous titters from someone at the very back of the hall. I smiled broadly to affirm the titterer. A few more people laughed. After that merriment spread like a forest fire. Monkeys! How absurd! Of course there was no such thing as a Gift of Monkeys – of course there wasn't! Ha-ha!

It was a close thing. Let's keep our ears and eyes wide open.

70

Persecution Foretold

13 : 9 – 13

'As for yourselves, beware; for they will hand you over to councils; and you will be beaten in synagogues; and you will stand before governors and kings because of me, as a testimony to them. And the good news must first be proclaimed to all nations. When they bring you to trial and hand you over, do not worry beforehand about what you are to say; but say whatever is given you at that time, for it is not you who speak, but the Holy Spirit. Brother will betray brother to death, and a father his child, and children will rise against parents and have them put to death; and you will be hated by all because of my name. But the one who endures to the end will be saved.

I AM NOT ONE OF LIFE'S NATURAL HEROES. SOME TIME AGO I was asked to write a poem or performance piece based on an old Bunyan hymn, the one that begins: 'He who would valiant be …'

He who would valiant be, let him come hither
Well, yes – quite
Absolutely
Let him come!
I'll be along in a minute
Not that I'm against hithering, you understand
I'm a hitherer
I am a hithering person – definitely am a potential one

177

It's just that – well, I've had to put the old hithering on hold
    for a bit
I suppose you could say I'm in the Slough of thing
Thingy
Things
The Slough of things
Couple of friendly bombs probably do the trick
Hmmm …
First avowed intent still intact, mind you
Oh, yes, to be – a proper one
To be a pilgrim
The thing is – modern pilgrimming doesn't quite hit the
    err …
Well, you know, the jolly old sort of churchy High thingy
    thing
Day off
Smart casual gear
Hope it doesn't rain
Who're you walking with?
Very profound experience
Has a very special meaning for me
Flowers are wonderful
Go every year
Usually get a coach together
Very good talk
Smashing meal
Charming little bed and breakfast.
Tidy prayers
Been happening for hundreds of years
That and the effort of the walking seems to add depth to it
Sort of thing
Nothing wrong with all that, of course
Nothing wrong
Very right
But …
Pilgrimming
Pilgrimming for me
Can we afford?
Did I remember?

I should have done it then
Oh, not again
All right, I'm sorry – I'm sorry – I'm sorry!
It didn't mean anything, honestly
I promise I won't
I promise I will
I promise I'll promise to promise that I'll promise anything
Someone at the door ...
Why the hell should I?
Why the hell shouldn't I?
Yes, of course I will – you know I will
Ow! Ow! My leg! Ow! Hurts too much to go on a pilgrimage ...
Sort of thing
Beset me round with dismal stories?
Dismal, abysmal – oh, yes! Oh, yes! Oh, yes!
My strength the more is?
No-o-o-o, no, no, no!
Well, look, never mind – we know we at the end shall life
    inherit
At least, we shall if -
Tell me, do your fancies seem to flee away?
Mine don't
Large, lazy, flightless birds, my fancies – like emus
They just run and run and run and run ...
Do you know, I really rather fear what men say
I suppose
The long and the short of it is – I do labour night and day
In a way
But
I'm not sure I've even begun
To be a pilgrim

Having read that you will understand why my heart fails me
when I read this passage about persecution. It always has. Since
becoming a Christian at the age of sixteen I have never lived
anywhere other than England, a nation where negative reactions
to the Christian faith rarely extend beyond scorn or aggressive
disagreement. That may well change. We are becoming – we

have become – a tiny minority in this country, and tiny minorities who do not stay comfortably in their allotted place tend not to be very popular.

In an age when the wide variety of religions and beliefs is popularly depicted as the result of a single spiritual light passing through each of the many different facets of a crystal, we Christians are not freed from our obligation to proclaim that Jesus is the way to heaven, that he wants to save the lives of the men and women for whom he died, and that we are his agents in attempting to bring this about.

'Live and let live,' would be the philosophy of most other religious groups. Sounds very sociable, rational and reasonable, doesn't it, until we reflect on the fact that if the Christian church adopted the same attitude we would actually be saying – to quote a James Bond title – 'Live and let die.'

So, the proverbial kitchen is likely to become rather hot in the near future. Will we get out? Or will we stay in? All the appalling things mentioned by Jesus in this passage, pain and betrayal and death and rejection, are heart-stopping prospects. What on earth would make it possible for us nervous travellers to endure such dreadful things, just as these disciples were to do, and just as countless Christians have done over the years?

The answer, of course, is that there is only one thing powerful enough to bring about this kind of miracle in failing pilgrims like you and I. Love is the answer. Not the gutless sentimentality endlessly portrayed by the commercial media of our day, but the kind of practical devotion that cares more for another than for itself and is prepared to sacrifice life itself if necessary.

When the bad times come, the way we cope will depend on how much we love Jesus, not on our natural coping skills. I am convinced that the primary study for each of us should be our relationship with him. Out of the treasure to be found in that nurtured relationship will come the courage and strength that we need, and as Jesus himself points out here, when the right time comes, even the words that we speak will be given to us.

71

The Desolating Sacrilege

13 : 14 – 23

'But when you see the desolating sacrilege set up where it ought
not to be (let the reader understand), then those in Judea must flee
to the mountains; the one on the housetop must not go down or
enter the house to take anything away; the one in the field must
not turn back to get a coat. Woe to those who are pregnant and to
those who are nursing infants in those days! Pray that it may not
be in winter. For in those days there will be suffering, such as has
not been from the beginning of the creation that God created until
now, no, and never will be. And if the Lord had not cut short those
days, no one would be saved; but for the sake of the elect, whom
he chose, he has cut short those days. And if anyone says to you at
that time, "Look! Here is the Messiah!" or "Look! There he
is!" — do not believe it. False messiahs and false prophets will
appear and produce signs and omens, to lead astray, if possible,
the elect. But be alert; I have already told you everything.'

THE URGENCY IN THESE WORDS IS UNMISTAKABLE. AND YET,
from time to time, cares of the world distract us from our
primary task of drawing as many as possible into the Kingdom
of God. Sometimes the Holy Spirit employs unpredictable,
tailor-made means to remind us of our priorities.

Take me, for instance. A year or two ago I had gone badly
off the boil as far as this sort of thing was concerned. Then, one
day, I was on the phone with a friend when I became aware
that, behind my back, water had started to pour from the hall
ceiling. Bidding my friend a hasty farewell and slamming the
phone down, I screamed hysterically up the stairs to let my wife
know what was happening, then wrenched open the pan drawer
in the kitchen, looking for receptacles large enough to catch the

flood that was cascading through and around the hall light-fitting from somewhere in our upstairs bathroom. This accomplished, I flung open the door that leads from the inside of our house to the garage, located the mains water tap and turned it firmly to the 'off' position.

Next, I steeled myself to perform the task I dreaded most. Finding the appropriate folder in the bowels of my study (a minor miracle) I called the emergency number that, if one was to believe the general tone of the blurb that caused us to sign up for the service in the first place, was certain to result in whole platoons of smart, friendly, efficient local plumbers screeching their vehicles to a halt in front of our house within five minutes at the very most. Having satisfied the professionally sceptical operative on the other end of the line that a vast amount of liquid escaping from the top half of our house into the bottom half was the sort of unplanned water-feature that might just creep into the 'emergency' category (that's why I dread such calls), I opened the front door so that no time should be lost when the first bright-eyed, eager plumber presented himself on our front step.

After a very long time I closed the front door because it was getting very cold. Nobody had arrived. Nobody had phoned. My wife had gone out to do something or other in Eastbourne. A great silence had descended over the damp and dripping house. Even our emergency had got bored and stopped pouring water into the hall. I knew that by the time our (theoretical) plumber did put in an appearance it would be a very unconvincing little emergency indeed. And I knew what he would do when he did eventually come. He would shake his head and suck air in through his teeth and tell me that he had just had to leave a multi-million pound job in order to attend my so-called emergency. He would tell me that it was no longer an emergency and then he would leave.

I was tempted to do nothing more because the water was no longer actually pouring through the ceiling, and getting a plumber to investigate the problem and fix it would be very expensive, and the chances were I'd never get round to claiming it on the house insurance, and anyway we'd got another bathroom so I could leave it for a while. So I probably would, and one of my sons would come home one day and, unaware of the problem lurking darkly there, would use the bathroom and the whole emergency would start all over again and I would kick myself for not having done something when I first became aware of the problem.

What had all this to do with the urgent need to spread the gospel? Ah, well, there is a small department of my brain that is permanently employed in making connections. It had made one.

A few days previously I had watched a television interview with a writer and theologian for whom I have the greatest respect. In this programme he was speaking about the most fundamental aspects of salvation. I agreed with everything that he said, but I found his use of language difficult. God, he said, is going to throw those people who are unrepentant and unbaptised into the equivalent of a hole in the ground, a rubbish tip, the sort of pit that used to lie just outside the city of Jerusalem two thousand years ago, a place mentioned by Jesus himself to illustrate this same point. The others, those who respond to the call of God, are to be 'recycled', and thereby made useful to God.

Personally, I felt that we were too close to the holocaust and, more recently, events in central Europe, to be able to stomach images of useless bodies being thrown into rubbish pits, and 'recycling' is the cold and mechanical terminology of the paper-mill and the car breakers-yard, not the language of a God who loves men and women so much that he sent his own son to offer us friendship and to illustrate his own vulnerability in such extraordinary parables as that of the Prodigal son.

There is a time for all things, though. The truth expressed in those harsh, utilitarian terms was an undeniable truth about the ever-present, cosmic emergency that faces every single individual born into this world. It is so tragically easy to forget the nail-biting urgency with which heaven awaits the return of each lost soul to the place where he or she really belongs. The means and the process have been well established, and, as I sat in my sodden house, I could not pretend that I was ignorant of them.

Opportunities to set people on the road for home do occur. Putting off those opportunities may have a far more fatal effect than the unexpected arrival of a few gallons of excess water. One day, I reflected, when we know the ultimate cost of such omissions, even the services of a plumber will seem cheap in comparison.

72

The Coming of the Son of Man

13 : 24 – 27

'But in those days, after that suffering, the sun will be darkened, and the moon will not give its light, and the stars will be falling from heaven, and the powers in the heavens will be shaken. Then they will see "the Son of Man coming in clouds" with great power and glory. Then he will send out the angels, and gather his elect from the four winds, from the ends of the earth to the ends of heaven.'

YES, THE CRUNCH WILL HAVE COME, AND EVERY SOUL WILL be answerable to the Son of Man. The language may have a bit of a Paramount Production feel about it, but the reality will be as dramatic as anyone could wish, and more so than some will cope with. Every human being is a case for emergency treatment until they have met their saviour. As we move through the gospel of Mark we are learning that this is what energised Jesus, and we are hoping and praying that, through his Spirit, it will energise us. I suppose some will still be alive when the great events described here take place, but the vast majority of us need to accept that only one thing in life is absolutely guaranteed, and that is the fact that we are going to die. I think you'll find the statistics are very clear on this subject.

You are more likely to die travelling by train than by plane
More likely to die in the winter than in the spring
More likely to die in a car-crash than from cancer
More likely to die watching East Enders than The Weakest Link
More likely to be murdered than to win the lottery
More likely to die in China than in Spain
You are more likely to die if you starve than if you eat
More likely to die at Old Trafford than in an ice-cream parlour
More likely to die in the morning than in the afternoon
More likely to die in Luton than in Milton Keynes
More likely to die in a Polish sentry-box than a Morris 1000 Traveller
More likely to die of cold than of heat
You are more likely to die in blue than in green
More likely to die in bed than in Birmingham
More likely to die intestate than on a tandem
More likely to die in company than alone
More likely to die on a Monday than on a Friday
More likely to die where you are than where you have been
You are more likely to die if you are tall than if you are short
More likely to die of hate than of love
More likely to die choking on a marble than to spontaneously combust
More likely to die facing south than facing east
More likely to die on land than on sea
More likely to die from leisure than from sport
You are more likely to die doing the twist than the jive
More likely to die at home than in any other place
More likely to die with friends than with strangers
More likely to die with an apology than with a blessing
More likely to die with a question than an answer
You are *most* likely to die if you are alive

The Lesson
of the Fig Tree

13 : 28 – 31

'From the fig tree learn its lesson: as soon as its branch becomes
tender and puts forth its leaves, you know that summer is near. So
also, when you see these things taking place, you know that he is
near, at the very gates. Truly I tell you, this generation will not pass
away until all these things have taken place. Heaven and earth will
pass away, but my words will not pass away.'

I IMAGINE THAT AT THIS POINT THE LEADER OF THE AUFT OR
Associated Union of Fig Trees might have decided it was time
for a little action.

'Do you think it right,' he would say, 'to curse one of our
less productive members just to make a point on one day, and
then, a few days later, get all mystical about the signs of summer that the vast majority of our members so consistently and
hardworkingly display being a metaphor for signs of the coming of the Son of Man? I ask you, is that *fair*? And before you
answer, I must warn you that we are a very powerful union. We
have branches everywhere …'

Heaven can't wait for me to arrive with my jokes.

Like Paul at a later date, Jesus seems to be saying that the
Second Coming is going to happen during the lifetime of his
own generation. In one sense, of course, it did. Jesus came back
to life after the crucifixion and appeared to large numbers of
people, including his own disciples. But that is not what Jesus
is talking about here. He is talking about the time when he will
make a dramatic and splendid return to collect those who

belong to him so that they – we – can be together in eternity. The final words of this passage are a reassurance for the disciples and for us that, whatever may happen either in heaven or on earth, the promises that Jesus makes to us will be kept. As we shall see, Jesus goes on to say that, in fact, even he is not allowed knowledge of when the day of his final return is to be. And it really does not matter which generation sees this great event in its own lifetime. The important things are that we shall be safe, that we shall be with him, and that it will be forever.

The Necessity for Watchfulness

13 : 32 – 37

'But about that day or hour no one knows, neither the angels in heaven, nor the Son, but only the Father. Beware, keep alert; for you do not know when the time will come. It is like a man going on a journey, when he leaves home and puts his slaves in charge, each with his work, and commands the doorkeeper to be on the watch. Therefore, keep awake — for you do not know when the master of the house will come, in the evening, or at midnight, or at cockcrow, or at dawn, or else he may find you asleep when he comes suddenly. And what I say to you I say to all: Keep awake.'

HERE, JESUS EMPHASISES THE POINT MADE IN THE PREVIOUS passage. Some mysteries we are allowed to solve, some we are not. The one about the time when the master of the house will return is indisputably one of the *nots*. Why do some folk find it so very difficult to accept this, despite Jesus' very clear words on the subject? Throughout the two thousand years since Jesus said these words, the church seems to have been constantly plagued by people telling us that the world is definitely going to come to an end at three-twenty-seven on the Tuesday after next. Is it a stage that some of us Christians' have to grow through? Do some of us unconsciously impose the development of personal faith upon the state of the world, confusing our own growing need for final resolution with a divine nudge to the effect that the end is very near? The problem with doing this is that those who believe it can be innoculated against a proper, balanced concern with both earth and heaven. In the final analysis people can say what they like, but it doesn't really matter. We do not know. We are not allowed to know. We are not going to know until the moment when it happens. It is a mystery.

As I said just now, though, we are allowed to solve some mysteries. Here is a strange little example. This was a long-standing mystery that I actually managed to solve. It concerned the man who sells newspapers from a little cabin at the bottom of the steps next to our local railway station.

A few years ago the whole of Polegate Station was relocated to a spot about a quarter of a mile up the line in a northerly direction. It now lies in the centre of town as opposed to a panic-stricken, sin-inducing, three minute sprint away from the nearest point where the Hailsham bus stops. Incidentally, I don't know who was responsible for planning this, but it must have been rather enjoyable, don't you think? Imagine being given a life-sized railway layout to play with, where you can simply command the station buildings to be lifted and moved along a bit. What fun!

Anyway, when the station moved, the married couple who sold sweets, newspapers, magazines, combs, tobacco and cigarettes to commuters from a little shop opposite the ticket-office moved with it. They were grey and elderly when I first met them back in the late seventies, so goodness knows how old they were at the time I'm writing about. I tended to encounter them early in the day, when, like so many newspaper sellers who begin their working stint before five o'clock in the morning, they were generally wearing warm scarves around their necks and fingerless woollen mittens on their hands. Despite the grinding nature of their daily occupation, they were a friendly couple who appeared to get on together very well. She was fitted with what seemed to be a purely ornamental hearing aid which probably helped. Physically creaky they may have been, but one sensed that in the case of these two people retirement would perhaps be nothing less than acquiescence in a sort of slow-motion decay. They were, quite simply, 'The People Who Did The Papers At The Station'. Long life and good health to them both, I said.

The mystery that I have mentioned was connected with the conversations I had over the years with the male half of this rather endearing double-act. Because I am like a retarded slug early in the morning, it actually took me years to focus on and identify the slightly strange nature of the exchanges that occurred between this ancient vendor and myself. How can I explain what I mean? Well, to put it bluntly, there was almost invariably one element in each of his conversations with me that made no sense at all. Here is a fairly typical example:

HIM : *(definitely addressing me as I enter the tiny cabin that is his shop)* That *is* the question they've got to ask themselves. If they don't – well, it's their funeral, don't you think?

ME : *(half asleep)* 'Daily Mail' please – and a comb. Shame about the football, eh?

HIM : *(handing me my change and shaking his head dolefully)* Should've picked Gazza, shouldn't they? Still the best we've got in my view.

ME : Thanks a lot. See you later – bye!

Do you see what I mean? That first comment of his floats wild and free like a solitary helium balloon. The onlooker, or in this case, the listener, has no idea where it has come from or where it is going. It just – is. But why?

The mystery of these unattached comments might have remained a mystery for ever if I had not hung about at the door of the little shop for a moment one day when I had a little more time than usual. The papers that morning had been full of the cricket-fixing scandal involving the captain of the South African team, and I had commented on the shocking nature of these revelations as I paid for my 'Daily Mail'.

'Well,' my friendly newspaper supplier had replied, 'nothing shocks me any more. And if you ask me, we haven't seen the last of it, not by a long chalk.'

I left, and a man passed me on his way into the shop as I lingered at the foot of the steps. A second later I clearly heard the shopkeeper address his new client.

'No,' he said, 'we haven't seen the last of it by a long chalk, not if you ask me. Shocking though, isn't it?'

My soul resonated with the fleeting instant of incomprehension that the new customer must have experienced at that point. I understood. The mystery was solved.

This newsagent had been doing his thing for so long that a subtle delusion had slowly taken root in his brain. You see, the clients who continually entered and vacated that little shop of his had merged and melded in his perception into a single universal client with whom he enjoyed an ongoing conversation throughout the morning. Thus, a verbal exchange with commuter 'A' was continued with bewildered commuter 'B' as though they were one and the same person. Puzzled commuter 'C' received the conversational baton relinquished by commuter 'B' and so on. There *was*, as it were, only one customer.

It's obvious when you know, isn't it?

When Jesus returns a lot of things are going to suddenly be very obvious. Instead of trying to predict the date, let's just make sure we're awake when he comes.

75

The Plot to Kill Jesus

14 : 1 – 2

It was two days before the Passover and the festival of Unleavened Bread. The chief priests and the scribes were looking for a way to arrest Jesus by stealth and kill him; for they said, 'Not during the festival, or there may be a riot among the people.'

THE IMPLICATION OF THESE WORDS IS A TRAGIC ONE, IS IT not? If the scribes had tried to arrest Jesus in public during the festival there would have been a huge outcry and they might well have failed to secure him. Yet, as we have already surmised in connection with the crowd that greeted him in Jerusalem, in a very short time, these people who were likely to riot on his behalf would be clamouring for his death in front of Pilate. That point has been made on so many occasions by so many people, but it is never any less full of sadness and darkness. The problem is that mobs are like that. Quite suddenly their allegiance or aggression can turn in an opposite direction and nobody is able to pinpoint the source of the change or identify the person who initiated it.

You see it happening with some kinds of birds and animals, don't you? Our house in Sussex looks out over pastureland, stretching for miles towards the sea. From time to time a huge flock of starlings will come wheeling over the valley, apparently intent on reaching some very definite objective. Suddenly, for no reason evident to the naked eye, the entire surging cloud of birds will swing with extraordinary uniformity in a completely different direction. How does that alteration begin? I have no idea.

The same thing happens, a lot less dramatically, with the

small herd of sheep that often occupies the field directly behind our house. When they are on the move they are more like one large sheep made up of lots of little ones than individual animals with minds of their own. You can occasionally observe four or five of these creatures trying to crush themselves into a hole or a gap that is never going to allow the passage of one sheep, let alone five of them trying to go through at the same time. They seem to suffer from an almost panic-stricken need to submerge their individuality in the flow of the common will.

Mobs are unstable and dangerous.

There has been a tendency in certain sections of the Christian church over the last twenty or thirty years to frown upon individuality as something that is not helpful to the body of Christ. The problem, as some people see it, is that major differences are divisive. The luxury of 'being yourself' is one that can only be indulged at the expense of brothers and sisters who want to lose themselves in the will of God. Ideally we would flatten out bumps and protrusions in the human terrain in order to facilitate ease of spiritual progress. There is something wilfully proud about an insistence on continuing to do or be what seems natural to you, a bit like a nun wearing a cowboy outfit in a convent.

If I was given incontrovertible evidence that God agreed with the people who say these things I think it might be back to the good old frog-worshipping for me. But I don't think I will ever see such evidence. I think of the Old Testament prophets, an array of singular, awkward, emotional, inspired characters. These men, chosen by God to speak out to the Israelites for him were certainly not selected for their willingness to toe the line and abandon eccentricities. I think of David, a great king, an adulterer and murderer, a loyal friend, a talented musician and lyricist, flawed and fantastic, at his best a man after God's own heart – a bit of an individual. I think of Saint Paul, fearsomely clever, as passionately committed to saving men and women for Christ as he had been to killing Christians, ingenious, hot-tempered, hardworking and as stubborn as they come. A conformist? Of course not. I think of Jesus himself. We have been meeting him in the pages of Mark's gospel. Does he strike you as one who would embrace or preach some kind of spiritual cloning philosophy?

Saint Paul gives us the best clue in his first letter to the Corinthians, where he uses the metaphor of a human body to explain the ideal relationship between members of the body of Christ:

> Now the body is not made up of one part but of many. If the foot should say, 'Because I am not a hand, I do not belong to the body,' it would not for that reason cease to be part of the body. And if the ear should say, 'Because I am not an eye, I do not belong to the body,' it would not for that reason cease to be part of the body. If the whole body were an eye, where would the sense of hearing be? If the whole body were an ear, where would the sense of smell be? But in fact God has arranged the parts in the body, every one of them, just as he wanted them to be. If they were all one part, where would the body be? As it is, there are many parts, but one body.
>
> The eye cannot say to the hand, 'I don't need you!' And the head cannot say to the feet, 'I don't need you!'

We in the Christian church are called, not to be a mindless mob, but a body of individuals, each contributing something unique and valuable to the whole, and each concerned for the welfare of the others.

76

The Anointing
at Bethany

14 : 3 – 9

While he was at Bethany in the house of Simon the leper, as he sat at the table, a woman came with an alabaster jar of very costly ointment of nard, and she broke open the jar and poured the ointment on his head.

But some were there who said to one another in anger, 'Why was the ointment wasted in this way? For this ointment could have been sold for more than three hundred denarii, and the money given to the poor.' And they scolded her.

But Jesus said, 'Let her alone; why do you trouble her? She has performed a good service for me. For you always have the poor with you, and you can show kindness to them whenever you wish; but you will not always have me. She has done what she could; she has anointed my body beforehand for its burial. Truly I tell you, wherever the good news is proclaimed in the whole world, what she has done will be told in remembrance of her.'

HERE, IN THIS WOMAN, WE SEE A FORERUNNER OF ALL those excellent people in the church who do apparently useless things for God, and get told off by people who think they know better. This woman wanted to do something extravagantly generous for Jesus because she loved him. 'Adoration' is not a term that is used a great deal in those parts of the church that I tend to frequent, but it describes what was happening here. She adored him and she wanted to give him a *great big treat*. It would be more than sad if the intensity of our good works (chance would be a fine thing!) distracted us from the need to simply adore Jesus in prayer and praise and worship and church decoration and artistic expression of all kinds and walks on the hills and half an hour in the garden and the strange enchantment that haloes humble sinners at the Communion rail.

Jesus must have so enjoyed the attentions of this lady. Tired and lonely, consistently placed either in the role of authority or healer or enemy, with pain and death rushing towards him now like a juggernaut, it would have been one of the very few moments in the course of his ministry when somebody had taken it upon themselves to do something lovely just for him, for no other reason than to make him happy. I wonder if it brought tears to his eyes for a moment. I would not be at all surprised.

The tradition of 'treats' is a very good one for us to maintain. Those church leaders with conscientious concern for the needs of others, those who are engaged in hard, materially unrewarding work for God, those who pray constantly and faithfully for their brothers and sisters, those who are always used because they are always available, those who look so strong that it seems impossible they should ever become weary and discouraged – give them a great big treat. Or a little treat. It could be anything from a doughnut to a holiday in the sun.

(The only thing I wouldn't recommend, and this is addressed to those who are neurotically attached to the notion that the Bible has to be followed with absolute accuracy, is breaking a jar of ointment over your friend's head without telling him or her you're going to do it. Times have changed. He or she might not like it.)

Go on – give someone a treat.

Judas Agrees to Betray Jesus

14 : 10 – 11

Then Judas Iscariot, who was one of the twelve, went to the chief priests in order to betray him to them. When they heard it, they were greatly pleased, and promised to give him money. So he began to look for an opportunity to betray him.

THE STORY OF JUDAS HAS ALWAYS HURT ME IN SOME OBSCURE way. I don't know if it should. It just does.

In Luke's gospel we hear Jesus telling Peter that Satan has asked to sift him, but that he, Jesus, has prayed for him so that his faith may not fail. As we shall see, Peter went on to deny his association with Jesus three times, and it was not until after the resurrection that he obeyed his master's command to turn back and strengthen his brothers. Jesus loved Peter. He prayed for him, and the prayer of the beloved Son of God was likely to be favourably received by his Father, wouldn't you say?

Did Jesus love Judas? Did Satan ask to sift Judas? Did Jesus say anything to Judas about his seemingly inevitable role? Did he try to dissuade Judas from betraying him? Did he know, even at the moment when he first called him, that Judas would one day sell him for thirty pieces of silver? Did Jesus pray for Judas, that he would change his mind and remain faithful, or was he just prophesy fodder? Does the fact that Judas was filled with remorse after committing his crime mean that he was forgiven even though Jesus said in John's gospel that he was doomed to destruction? When, as Peter tells us, Jesus went down to preach to the souls in hell, was Judas there, tearfully cowering in a corner? Did he come to the front when it was time for the altar-call? Did he make a new commitment? Will we meet Judas in heaven? If not, is it fair? Why am I going if he's not? Am I making God angry by asking all these questions?

78

The Passover
with the Disciples

14 : 12 – 21

On the first day of Unleavened Bread, when the Passover lamb is sacrificed, his disciples said to him, 'Where do you want us to go and make the preparations for you to eat the Passover?'

So he sent two of his disciples, saying to them, 'Go into the city, and a man carrying a jar of water will meet you; follow him, and wherever he enters, say to the owner of the house, "The Teacher asks, Where is my guest room where I may eat the Passover with my disciples?" He will show you a large room upstairs, furnished and ready. Make preparations for us there.'

So the disciples set out and went to the city, and found everything as he had told them; and they prepared the Passover meal.

When it was evening, he came with the twelve. And when they had taken their places and were eating, Jesus said, 'Truly I tell you, one of you will betray me, one who is eating with me.'

They began to be distressed and to say to him one after another, 'Surely, not I?'

He said to them, 'It is one of the twelve, one who is dipping bread into the bowl with me. For the Son of Man goes as it is written of him, but woe to that one by whom the Son of Man is betrayed! It would have been better for that one not to have been born.'

PEOPLE SOMETIMES TALK AS THOUGH THE BUSINESS OF THE man with the jar of water, and the ready-furnished upstairs room was a miracle. I grant that it might have been. As we have seen, divisions between the natural and the miraculous in the life and ministry of Jesus were not always clear-cut. On the other hand, it may have been a special arrangement that the master had made with one of his wealthier supporters in Jerusalem.

I was intrigued by something I read in 'Jack', that wonderfully warm biography of C. S. Lewis written by George Sayer, one of his closest friends. Until a very late stage in his long relationship with Sayer, Lewis never once mentioned or referred to Arthur Greeves, his lifelong friend and correspondent in Ireland. The same was true for many others who thought they had known Lewis intimately. This strategy of compartmentalising friends and associates may well have been one that was adopted by Jesus. Who, for instance, owned the house in which he met the Syrophoenician woman? How many people were familiar with the 'bolthole' where friendship with Lazarus and his household offered rare opportunities to relax? How were those two disciples that we met earlier able to take an unridden colt away from its owners simply by saying that the master had need of it? Jesus was one of the first great 'networkers', as are many of his followers today. He mixed with rich and poor, famous and infamous, and must have attracted loyalty and a desire to serve him from both (remember, Jairus was a leader of the synagogue, and there cannot have been much he would not have done for the man who brought his daughter back to life).

By the way, I can't help wondering if Jesus appointed the same pair of spiritual heroes to undertake this mission as he had sent to fetch the colt. If so, I suppose they might have been just a tad more confident this time. Or was it just that, by now, they had all learned to believe that when Jesus said something, it was so?

Speaking of which, here is a question about this passage. Why did disciple after disciple ask if he was the one who would betray Jesus? I mean – they knew, didn't they? Judas knew he would and the others knew they would not. Surely. So why did they ask? There are only two explanations that I can think of.

One is that they had all, from time to time, harboured the temptation to make a little money by handing Jesus over to the authorities. I just do not believe that, do you? Peter, for instance, may have fallen apart later, when all the traditional means of defending his friend had been dismissed as useless – but selling his master for cash? I don't think so. That's not the explanation. Judas was the only one with that on his mind.

No, I think the answer goes back to what I said just now. Experience had taught these fellows that when Jesus made an assertion it was unvaryingly correct. In a way it's rather sweet, isn't it? They knew they had no intention of betraying their master, but he had said one of them would, so – well, perhaps in some way they hadn't understood – they would!

'Is it me?'

'No.'

'Phew!'

79

The Institution
of the Lord's Supper

14 : 22 – 25

While they were eating, he took a loaf of bread, and after blessing it he broke it, gave it to them, and said, 'Take; this is my body.'

Then he took a cup, and after giving thanks he gave it to them, and all of them drank from it. He said to them, 'This is my blood of the covenant, which is poured out for many. Truly I tell you, I will never again drink of the fruit of the vine until that day when I drink it new in the kingdom of God.'

THESE WORDS, THE THOUGHT OF ACTUALLY TAKING COMMUNION, and communion itself, always make my mouth water. I'm afraid this is partly for a very basic and human reason. There is nothing more calculated to tickle your taste buds and get your gastric juices flowing than restricted, tiny amounts of something you really enjoy. It happens in the supermarket sometimes, doesn't it? They put out a plastic box filled with little cubes of cheese on the deli-counter, and I can never resist having a taste. Perhaps because the diced portions are so miniscule, they usually seem to taste heavenly, and I quite often end up buying half a pound and wishing later that I hadn't. Mouthfuls don't always match up to morsels. A very tiny sip of wine and a fragment of bread have exactly the same effect, except that, in the case of wine particularly, experience has shown a whole glass of the same liquid is unlikely to disappoint.

Much more importantly, but in a closely linked way, Communion makes my mouth water in a symbolic and spiritual sense as well. There is something profoundly exciting, tantalising, moving, awe-inspiring, ineffably reassuring about tasting the bread of the love of God, about sipping at the sweet wine of salvation, about being allowed to take into one's body a very special share of the knowledge that, two millennia ago, the Servant King gave his body and blood so that we can be with him for ever.

Mysterious, impenetrable, wonderful.

80

Peter's Denial Foretold

14 : 26 – 31

When they had sung the hymn, they went out to the Mount of Olives. And Jesus said to them, 'You will all become deserters; for it is written,

'I will strike the shepherd, and the sheep will be scattered.' But after I am raised up, I will go before you to Galilee.'

Peter said to him, 'Even though all become deserters, I will not.'

Jesus said to him, 'Truly I tell you, this day, this very night, before the cock crows twice, you will deny me three times.'

But he said vehemently, 'Even though I must die with you, I will not deny you.'

And all of them said the same.

THERE WAS NEVER ANYTHING REMOTELY SENTIMENTAL ABOUT the Son of God, was there? After the warmth and togetherness of that final passover meal, an occasion that must have been shot through with grief for Jesus for a number of reasons, he has no hesitation in dropping a Monty Python boot on the situation by telling the disciples exactly what is about to happen. Buoyed up and filled with confidence by the solidarity that tends to be engendered by such communal events, the last thing they would have expected was to be told that they would shortly desert their master and run off like a flock of frightened sheep. No doubt they felt rather hurt. Why did Jesus place so little trust in them?

In fact, of course, Jesus was not so much expressing an opinion as stating a fact. He knew the strengths and weaknesses of these men, and on a purely human level he could certainly have predicted how each of them was likely to behave under pressure. But, that aside, this was Holy Spirit knowledge, spoken in harmony with the rhythms of scripture. They would desert him. It was inevitable.

It seems important to me to bear in mind that the disciples were absolutely sincere in what they said. They had no intention of deserting Jesus, and, as we shall see when the crowd with clubs and swords comes to arrest him, one of his followers (Peter, according to John's gospel), is quite prepared to draw his own sword and 'have a go'. Sincere but misguided.

One of the most difficult lessons we followers of Jesus have to learn is that the strength or sincerity of our feelings and intentions is not a reliable guide to the thing God actually wants us to do. I may, in a sudden burst of enthusiasm, vow to God that I will take on an evening job in order to raise more money for the poor, but if what he actually wants is for me to ring the bell of every house in my street and share the gospel with whoever answers the door, I may well be wasting my time. Or the other way round.

Isn't it hard to give up our pet certainties? Paul summed it up in his comment to the Corinthians:

> You are not your own;
> you were bought at a price.

It takes a lifetime to learn.

81

Jesus Prays in Gethsemane

14 : 32 – 42

They went to a place called Gethsemane; and he said to his disciples, 'Sit here while I pray.'

He took with him Peter and James and John, and began to be distressed and agitated. And he said to them, 'I am deeply grieved, even to death; remain here, and keep awake.'

And going a little farther, he threw himself on the ground and prayed that, if it were possible, the hour might pass from him. He said, 'Abba, Father, for you all things are possible; remove this cup from me; yet, not what I want, but what you want.'

He came and found them sleeping; and he said to Peter, 'Simon, are you asleep? Could you not keep awake one hour? Keep awake and pray that you may not come into the time of trial; the spirit indeed is willing, but the flesh is weak.'

And again he went away and prayed, saying the same words. And once more he came and found them sleeping, for their eyes were very heavy; and they did not know what to say to him.

He came a third time and said to them, 'Are you still sleeping and taking your rest? Enough! The hour has come; the Son of Man is betrayed into the hands of sinners. Get up, let us be going. See, my betrayer is at hand.'

SPRING WAS COMING. THE MORNING SUN LOBBED GENTLY bouncing dappled patterns onto the walls and flat surfaces in my study.

The approaching season was my consolation as I sat there buried in piles of paper, notes on the wall reminding me of deadlines, and the unanswered letters that, like the poor, are always with me. On that day I had to write an article, do a final tidy-up of my latest book before sending it off to the publishers, get all my stuff ready for a two-day speaking tour in the Midlands, and get to the bank to do the regular financial juggling act between three accounts that allows the bank and me to believe that, in some mystical way, I *am* in credit.

Spring was coming. The air was a cocktail of light and life.

It comforted me as I re-read the article that had appeared in a Dutch newspaper a couple of weeks earlier. It included a photograph of me looking like a giant walrus standing on its hind legs, and it described me in such a way that, if I had had small children, I would certainly not have allowed them near me. I have always had difficulty with innocent, if ill-advised comments on the extreme narrowness of my eyes. The man who wrote this article has gone just a little further. He depicted me as a shambling, egg-stained, tramp-like barrage balloon, lurching wretchedly around the world in strange green trousers, mumbling through his stubble and tearing raw meat apart with his bare hands. The article went on to speak very favourably about the books I have written and the things that I was saying, but I'm afraid I suffer from recurrent bouts of humanness. So, would I have preferred an article which damned my ministry but said I looked great? Yes! Yes! A thousand times yes! What do *you* think? Naturally, I forgave the man who wrote about me like this. I had to. I'm a Christian.

Spring was coming. Outside my window emerald grass gleamed in the early April sunshine.

This was no consolation at all in that particular year to hundreds of farmers all over Great Britain, men and women whose lives had been bound up with the animals that were being slaughtered in huge numbers every day because of Foot and Mouth disease. And it was not just about money. It was about watching helplessly as your identity, the evidence of who and what you were, went up in smoke – literally. Make no mistake, hearts were being broken by the spread of that dreadful disease, and seemed to go on and on. Shepherds move heaven and earth to save one lost sheep, but those people were losing every single one.

Spring was coming. Daffodils and crocuses brought natural neon from the dark earth.

No help at all to the old friend who knocked on my door just a few minutes after I finally finished writing that article. Her husband of over twenty years had informed her that he had been having an affair for fifteen of those years. He had gone, leaving his wife to look back on one and a half decades of lies and deceit, to wonder how she and her daughter and son would ever close such a deep and unexpected wound in the softest and most vulnerable part of their lives. She was stiff with pain. I prayed that she would know the presence of the suffering God as she struggled in that terrible place.

Spring was coming. Clouds blustered through skies as serenely blue as a hedge-sparrow's egg.

It was a joy to me as I approached my fifty-second year to see how such simple pleasures as the alternating of the seasons had moved so close to the top of my personal list of priorities. Whatever I lost or gained in material terms, I was the grateful recipient of these timeless benefits, dramas of change in colour and mood and texture and temperature. Spring was an early birthday present from God. He had given it to me at this time in every year of my life, and I was only just beginning to realise how valuable it was.

Spring was coming. Jesus had risen!

Soon we would eat chocolate eggs and sing Easter hymns and celebrate the death and resurrection of Jesus. It occurred to me that you would have to be blind or obtuse to miss all the references to the natural world in the sayings and teachings of Jesus. We often talk about the sacrifice that Jesus made for our sakes in going to the cross, but there is one aspect of that great sacrifice that had never struck me as forcibly as it did on that particular morning. Jesus remained obedient at Gethsemane. He died at the age of thirty-three.

He gave up so many springtimes for me.

82

The Betrayal
and Arrest of Jesus

14 : 43 – 52

Immediately, while he was still speaking, Judas, one of the twelve, arrived; and with him there was a crowd with swords and clubs, from the chief priests, the scribes, and the elders. Now the betrayer had given them a sign, saying, 'The one I will kiss is the man; arrest him and lead him away under guard.' So when he came, he went up to him at once and said, 'Rabbi!' and kissed him. Then they laid hands on him and arrested him. But one of those who stood near drew his sword and struck the slave of the high priest, cutting off his ear.

Luke 22 : 51

But Jesus answered, 'No more of this!' And he touched the man's ear and healed him.

Then Jesus said to them, 'Have you come out with swords and clubs to arrest me as though I were a bandit? Day after day I was with you in the temple teaching, and you did not arrest me. But let the scriptures be fulfilled.'

All of them deserted him and fled. A certain young man was following him, wearing nothing but a linen cloth. They caught hold of him, but he left the linen cloth and ran off naked.

I HAVE INCLUDED THE EXTRA VERSE FROM ANOTHER GOSPEL for the indulgent reason that it is one of my favourite moments in any of the gospels and I might never get the chance to write about Luke.

Here are two memories that strike me as I read these words for the umpteenth time.

The first memory, one I have recorded elsewhere, is of my second son, Joe, casting a large metal 'spoon' in the direction of a lake in New Zealand and catching me in the ear in the process. The actual moment when the hook made contact felt as if a brick had hit me on the side of the head. One of the three barbed hooks in this device managed to go straight through the lobe of my left ear, so that I arrived at the local clinic a few minutes later with what appeared to be a large, green metallic earring dangling from my ear. I had to give the doctor permission to laugh or he might well have burst.

The second is of a piece of film that was shown on the news a year or so before Nelson Mandela's release from prison. Archbishop Desmond Tutu was conducting a service or leading a meeting from a platform in one of the South African townships. In the middle of these proceedings a man was led into the space in front of the platform with a car tyre around his neck and his hands tied behind his back. He was about to be subjected to that appalling practice known as 'necklacing', where the victim suffers an indescribably awful death by having the rubber tyre around his neck set alight and left to burn until he is dead. I have no idea what crime this man was supposed to have committed. Presumably it was some act of treachery against the community. When Tutu saw what was happening he immediately stopped what he was doing and reached down to haul the man up onto the platform beside him. However righteous and justified such barbaric treatment might have seemed to others, Tutu, who is a follower of Jesus, saw only the need for compassion and rescue. That moment and this moment of aggression and healing recorded in the gospels meet in a perfect circle.

This chap, then, the slave of the high priest, would have been conscious of something scything through the near-darkness in his direction. Perhaps he instinctively moved his head to one side, and thereby saved his life. Instead of his whole body being sliced neatly in two, his ear was cut off. It must have felt as though three or four large bricks had landed on the side of his head at the same time. In the confusion of the moment did he even know that his ear had been sliced away?

And then comes this strange, strange moment, when Jesus, his face contracted with concern and compassion even in the midst of this, the darkest hour of his life so far, reaches out his hand, and, rather like a magician taking an egg from behind someone's head, heals the man almost before he is aware that healing is needed.

No wonder Peter ran away.

(Incidentally, one day I would like to ask Jesus if he picked up the severed ear and, as it were, stuck it back on. Or did he create a new one? If that bewildered slave had walked dazedly through Gethsemane on the following morning, would he have come across a grisly reminder of the night before – his *old* ear?)

The mark of the man and of the God. After a night of terrible fear and apprehension, he finds that a gang of men, led by one of his beloved disciples, has come with clubs and swords to drag him to his death, and when one of those same men is injured, he instantly responds from a heart of genuine compassion and care. The pattern of his love for us. A wonderful saviour.

83

Jesus before
the Council

14 : 53 – 65

They took Jesus to the high priest; and all the chief priests, the elders, and the scribes were assembled. Peter had followed him at a distance, right into the courtyard of the high priest; and he was sitting with the guards, warming himself at the fire.

Now the chief priests and the whole council were looking for testimony against Jesus to put him to death; but they found none. For many gave false testimony against him, and their testimony did not agree.

Some stood up and gave false testimony against him, saying, 'We heard him say, "I will destroy this temple that is made with hands, and in three days I will build another, not made with hands."'

But even on this point their testimony did not agree.

Then the high priest stood up before them and asked Jesus, 'Have you no answer? What is it that they testify against you?'

But he was silent and did not answer. Again the high priest asked him, 'Are you the Messiah, the Son of the Blessed One?'

Jesus said, 'I am; and "you will see the Son of Man seated at the right hand of the Power," and "coming with the clouds of heaven."'

Then the high priest tore his clothes and said, 'Why do we still need witnesses? Have you heard his blasphemy! What is your decision?'

All of them condemned him as deserving death. Some began to spit on him, to blindfold him, and to strike him, saying to him, 'Prophesy!' The guards also took him over and beat him.

I WAS ONCE INVITED TO SIT IN ON A JEWISH DISCUSSION GROUP in a synagogue, led by a friend of mine who is a rabbi. A large part of the discussion centred on the forthcoming festival of Passover, and the origin and meaning of various aspects of the traditional meal that is the central feature of these celebrations. One aspect of this meal that had always intrigued me was the setting of a place and a vacant chair for Elijah. At one point in the meal a glass of wine is poured for the prophet and someone, usually one of the children, gets up to open the door of the room in case Elijah is waiting outside to come in. Traditionally, as we have been reminded in our reading of Mark's gospel, the return of Elijah is a sure sign that the Messiah is about to appear.

When I was told that questions would be in order I knew exactly what I wanted to ask.

'Do any of you believe,' I queried tentatively, 'that the day will come when someone will go to the door and Elijah *will* be there, and he'll come in and sit at his place and drink his glass of wine? Will he really come back one day to tell you that the Messiah is on his way? What do you think?'

Much puzzlement and head scratching. Many groups of Christians would react in the same way if you asked them to describe the working of the Holy Spirit in their lives, or how they picture the Second Coming. My Jewish friends said that they had never considered such a question before. It was a *good* question, they added, after giving the matter a little thought, but not one that had ever occurred to them in the past. Yes, a *very* good question.

This is the trouble with tradition, symbolism and ceremony, isn't it? Such things are enriching and helpful as long as they do not cause the truth to be atrophied and made separate from the real world. Remember Peter and the Transfiguration?

I wonder if anyone on this council that condemned Jesus actually believed that a Messiah was coming one day. Or had such a formal, religious crust formed around the prospect that it had ceased to be regarded as a living possibility? Apart from anything else, if claiming to be the Messiah was to be regarded as such abundant proof that the person claiming to be the Messiah was definitely *not* the Messiah, how on earth would the real Messiah ever manage to identify himself?

Just think of it! He was standing there in front of them, the real Messiah, the Son of God, the one they claimed to be waiting for, and they were blind to the truth. They said he deserved to die, and spat at him and sent him out to be beaten by the guards.

Words and patterns and traditions can easily become stale. It happens to the best and the worst of us. From time to time we need to look at what we say we believe, and ask ourselves if those beliefs are still warm and alive in us. What a shame if we were to discover that someone had been waiting for us to open the door at the very time when we least expected it. What a shame if we missed him because our attention was elsewhere.

Peter Denies Jesus

14 : 66 – 72

While Peter was below in the courtyard, one of the servant-girls of the high priest came by. When she saw Peter warming himself, she stared at him and said, 'You also were with Jesus, the man from Nazareth.'

But he denied it, saying, 'I do not know or understand what you are talking about.' And he went out into the forecourt.

Then the cock crowed.

And the servant-girl, on seeing him, began again to say to the bystanders, 'This man is one of them.' But again he denied it. Then after a little while the bystanders again said to Peter, 'Certainly you are one of them; for you are a Galilean.'

But he began to curse, and he swore an oath, 'I do not know this man you are talking about.'

At that moment the cock crowed for the second time. Then Peter remembered that Jesus had said to him, 'Before the cock crows twice, you will deny me three times.' And he broke down and wept.

THIS PASSAGE ALWAYS BRINGS TEARS TO MY EYES, AND I HAVE already written too much about it in the past.

All I will say is that almost all useful Christians have undergone serious heart surgery. A large part of the reason for that is the need for us to experience what it means to be utterly helpless and completely dependent on the strength, gentleness and skill in the hands of the surgeon. Here is Peter, stretched out on the operating table, weeping over his insoluble problems of weakness and need. Big rocks don't cry? Oh, yes – they do. Indeed they do.

Jesus before Pilate

15 : 1 – 5

As soon as it was morning, the chief priests held a consultation with the elders and scribes and the whole council. They bound Jesus, led him away, and handed him over to Pilate.

Pilate asked him, 'Are you the King of the Jews?'

He answered him, 'You say so.'

Then the chief priests accused him of many things.

Pilate asked him again, 'Have you no answer? See how many charges they bring against you.'

But Jesus made no further reply, so that Pilate was amazed.

Read in isolation, passages like this may give the impression that Jesus, in some way, gave up in the end. We have always had to struggle as a church with the quite commonly held perception of Jesus as a limp, flower-clutching, hippy-like figure, who believed there was some benefit in letting people walk all over him. Of course, anyone who has actually read the New Testament would find it difficult, if not impossible, to sustain this view. The strong, emotional, unsentimental personality that is revealed to us in the four gospels is about as far removed from that false image as it is possible to be. Such items of teaching as praying for your enemies and loving your neighbour are strategies in the forward movement of the gospel, not evidences of a tendency to retreat or give up. Matthew records how, after healing the slave's ear in the garden, Jesus makes the point that, if he wanted, he could call on twelve legions of angels to defend him. But that was not what was needed if the job was to be done properly.

In any case, any aspects of Jesus ministry and teaching that might appear weak or non-aggressive must be set against a multitude of events and warnings that reveal the uncompromising toughness of the Son of God. If you will excuse me a quick burst of irony, here, for those who still nurture the illusion that Jesus was a softy, is a sermon that he certainly did not preach on the Mount or anywhere else.

> Blessed are they who exchange money and sell cattle, sheep or doves in the temple court, for they shall be driven out with a knotted cord.
>
> Blessed is the fig tree when it bears no fruit, for it shall be cursed and it shall die.
>
> Blessed are they who cause little ones to sin, for it will be better for them if they were to drown with a millstone tied around their necks.
>
> Blessed are they who blaspheme against the Holy Spirit, for they can never be forgiven.
>
> Blessed are they whose debts have been cancelled, but will not cancel the debts owed to them, for they shall be turned over to the jailers to be tortured until they have paid back all that they owe.
>
> Blessed are they who arrive to celebrate the wedding of the king's son without wedding clothes, for they shall be bound hand and foot and thrown outside into the darkness, where there will be weeping and gnashing of teeth.
>
> Blessed are they who say to me, 'Lord, Lord', but do not do the will of my Father, for they will not enter the kingdom of heaven.
>
> Blessed are many who will protest to me, 'Did we not prophesy in your name, and in your name drive out many demons and perform many miracles?', for I will tell them plainly, 'I never knew you. Away from me, you evildoers!'

Blessed are they who refuse to forgive others, for they will not be forgiven by God.

Blessed are they who continue to sin after being rescued from the cruelty of men, for worse shall befall them.

Blessed are they who love to pray standing in the synagogues and on the street corners to be seen by men, for they have received their reward in full.

Blessed are they who judge others, for they will be judged by the same measure.

Blessed are they who did not give me something to eat when I was hungry, nor something to drink when I was thirsty, who did not invite me in when I was a stranger, nor clothe me when I was naked, nor visit me in prison when I was sick, for they will depart into the eternal fire prepared for the devil and his angels.

Blessed are they who do not believe in me, for they shall not inherit eternal life.

86

Pilate Hands Jesus over to Be Crucified

15 : 6 – 15

Now at the festival he used to release a prisoner for them, anyone for whom they asked. Now a man called Barabbas was in prison with the rebels who had committed murder during the insurrection. So the crowd came and began to ask Pilate to do for them according to his custom.

Then he answered them, 'Do you want me to release for you the King of the Jews?' For he realized that it was out of jealousy that the chief priests had handed him over.

But the chief priests stirred up the crowd to have him release Barabbas for them instead.

Pilate spoke to them again, 'Then what do you wish me to do with the man you call the King of the Jews?'

They shouted back, 'Crucify him!'

Pilate asked them, 'Why, what evil has he done?'

But they shouted all the more, 'Crucify him!'

So Pilate, wishing to satisfy the crowd, released Barabbas for them; and after flogging Jesus, he handed him over to be crucified.

WORSE THAN A HITCHCOCK FILM. THAT FLOCK OF STARLINGS we mentioned earlier has turned in a completely different direction, and the dark cloud of death is about to settle on Jesus as a result.

Why did the crowd turn so violently against a man who had entertained and healed them, ministered to their needs, and shown the way to eternal life? This passage indicates that the chief priests worked as hard as they could to influence the popular decision about whose release should be called for, but how was it possible for them to have such a dramatic effect?

Last night I was watching a repeat of one of those television programmes featuring David Blaine, who describes himself as an entertainer, his particular field being street magic. All of the illusions in last night's programme were performed to ordinary people he encountered on pavements or in other public places. As well as being a colossally talented conjurer, Blaine seems to have an instinctive understanding of human beings, and a style that is almost mystical in its intensity. As I watched I found it interesting to see how members of the public reacted to what they were seeing and experiencing.

For a start most of them were delighted at what they saw. A profoundly skilled illusionist excavates our sense of what is possible and impossible, awaking us to reality and the rules that normally govern day-to-day living. These people were delighting in the apparent juggling of those rules.

Secondly they were quite amazed. Some of David Blaine's illusions are so inexplicable that they have a stunning effect. No doubt other conjurors would say that he is simply dishing up old tricks in new forms. I know nothing about that. All I can say is that these people judged the new forms to be pretty staggering. I agreed with them.

Thirdly, and most interesting of all, there was no doubt that some of the 'victims' were actually frightened. In one or two cases indulgent smiles and expressions of bright expectancy were abruptly replaced with genuinely troubled frowns as the people concerned struggled to mentally accommodate what looked to them like a clear defiance of logic. On some important level they just didn't like it. One or two actually moved or even ran out of the situation as if wishing to distance themselves from their own incomprehension.

Parallels with the ministry of Jesus are interesting. (There is no need to be offended by the comparison. Who, after all, could possibly be more transparently honest than the man who proclaims himself an illusionist?) Jesus never performed magic, but he did perform miracles as he walked the highways and byways of Judea, and the gospels leave us in no doubt that the crowds were delighted and amazed by his authority, his teaching and his use of supernatural powers. In addition, as we saw in the case of the Gerasene demoniac for example, the locals were terrified by what had happened and begged Jesus to leave. We have previously seen, in connection with the Pharisees' response to the healing of the man with the withered hand, that there can be a terror of exchanging one form of solid ground for another, and it may have been this very human vulnerability that the chief priests so successfully exploited on this occasion. I fear that we all tend to be experts on our own weaknesses when we observe them in others.

This fear of commitment to full immersion in the divine will and ways of Jesus is something that you and I really do have to overcome if we are to walk usefully with him. At some point it may involve a step into darkness or insecurity that will truly frighten us, and we cannot know or understand the relief and safety that awaits us on the other side of abandonment until that step has been taken.

The Soldiers Mock Jesus

15 : 16 – 20

Then the soldiers led him into the courtyard of the palace (that is, the governor's headquarters) ; and they called together the whole cohort. And they clothed him in a purple cloak; and after twisting some thorns into a crown, they put it on him. And they began saluting him, 'Hail, King of the Jews!' They struck his head with a reed, spat upon him, and knelt down in homage to him. After mocking him, they stripped him of the purple cloak and put his own clothes on him. Then they led him out to crucify him.

THESE ROMAN SOLDIERS TAKE THEIR PLACE IN A SEEMINGLY endless procession of people who, throughout history, have believed that physical domination will automatically crush the spirit of any man or woman. For a short time this band of men were not prevented by God from mocking and assaulting his son. Their 'joke' centred on the fact that this helpless wretch who had so foolishly claimed to be a king, was visibly, pathetically bereft of all the powers normally associated with royalty. It was a bit of fun for the six-hundred or so lads in the cohort, and it makes me feel sick.

I have heard it said recently that well over one hundred thousand Christians are martyred every year in this present age. This means that, at the very moment you are reading these words there will be followers of Jesus undergoing the same brutal treatment as that endured by their master. Why not take time now to pray for one anonymous man, woman or child who is suffering in that way? We cannot know the name of our brother or sister, and they will certainly not know us, but God will know, and it will be worth doing. In some dank and love-less cell thousands of miles away our prayers might be tiny points of light in the darkness. Perhaps we will continue to pray for that one person. If so it will be like adopting someone whom we shall never see or meet on this side of heaven. Who knows what might be possible in the lives of those people through our prayers?

The Crucifixion of Jesus

15 : 21 – 32

They compelled a passer-by, who was coming in from the country, to carry his cross; it was Simon of Cyrene, the father of Alexander and Rufus.

Then they brought Jesus to the place called Golgotha (which means the place of a skull). And they offered him wine mixed with myrrh; but he did not take it. And they crucified him, and divided his clothes among them, casting lots to decide what each should take. It was nine o'clock in the morning when they crucified him. The inscription of the charge against him read, 'The King of the Jews.' And with him they crucified two bandits, one on his right and one on his left.

Those who passed by derided him, shaking their heads and saying, 'Aha! You who would destroy the temple and build it in three days, save yourself, and come down from the cross!'

In the same way the chief priests, along with the scribes, were also mocking him among themselves and saying, 'He saved others;

he cannot save himself. Let the Messiah, the King of Israel, come
down from the cross now, so that we may see and believe.'
Those who were crucified with him also taunted him.

Here is the stark record of what must have appeared a total disaster to the eleven disciples and all the others who had followed Jesus before his arrest.

As I write these words hundreds of thousands of people are trying to recover from and make sense of another disaster. It was just two weeks ago that the terrorist attack on New York, Washington and Pittsburgh left thousands dead, a nation in shock, and a world in fear of what the future might bring. In one sense I don't suppose the dust will ever really settle. However many tons of rubble are cleared, for those whose loved ones have been snatched away there will always be a black cloud pressing down over the month of September, over New York or Washington or Pittsburgh, over America as it now is, over all the pain-wracked obligations attending survival and the need to continue living.

I didn't lose anyone I loved. I shed a lot of warm tears for those who had.

Turning for support towards the structure of my faith in God on that dreadful Tuesday in 2001, I found that something in the nature of a small explosion had happened there as well. Wondering dazedly through the wreckage I picked up spars and supports that might have seemed just what was needed in the days when this kind of disaster was purely hypothetical.

Pray for your enemies.
Do not return evil for evil.
Be angry but do not sin.
All things work together for ...

I flung these charred fragments from me as the estimate of fatalities rose by the hour and images of death, anguish and unbearable loss filled our screens in a mosaic of horror and hopelessness.

Why?

I remembered an occasion when this same brief question was asked. The disciples wanted to know why a man encountered on the road had been born blind, a tragic enough disaster for that individual. Was it his or his parents' sin that was being punished with the affliction?

'It was neither,' replied Jesus, 'but because of his blindness you will see God perform a miracle for him.'

'So what exactly,' I demanded hotly, 'is the nature of the miracle you are planning to perform for America and the world in this ghastly situation. How will the glory of God be manifested through this nightmare of fear and blood and bodies and bits of bodies and shattered families and uncontainable grief?'

I was as blind as that man was before Jesus healed him. As my sight returned I saw and still see something overwhelmingly beautiful taking root and flowering in the very ashes of this conflagration. I saw men and women performing heroic, sacrificial acts of love and kindness towards each other, I heard of the support and friendship of groups and nations all over the world. I sensed the unity of sympathy and goodwill pervading a large part of the international community. Very specially, it was as though, for a time at least, Americans in general and inhabitants of New York and Washington in particular had had the best and most compassionate elements of their humanity forced to the surface of their everyday lives. Against one of the darkest and most evil backgrounds one could imagine, this multi-coloured bloom of goodness was vivid and alive.

It was also the case that people were asking each other hard, vital questions about life and death and love and the meaning of existence. These kinds of enquiries are roads along which many a weary and troubled prodigal might travel towards the truth and reality for which they search.

All of these things constitute a miracle that might ultimately be more satisfying than revenge.

But what of the thirst for revenge? Well, yes. When part of you has been torn away with heartless violence, why would you not want revenge? Why would you not desire to see the persons responsible paying the penalty for their crimes? I could see the need for action that would not only bring justice for those who had died and suffered, but would also deter terrorists from carrying out attacks in the future. These things had to be done with wisdom and appropriate restraint, but they had to be done.

Those of us who follow Jesus were obliged to remember, however, that the terrorist mastermind who planned that atrocity is but a ghost-writer, for the true author of evil is Satan, and his most consummate wish is that evil should beget evil. We must never allow him that satisfaction.

There was no easy comfort at that time. There never is on such occasions. But there are two things that might be worth saying.

First, when I think of those who lost wives, husbands, parents, children and friends, I remember that strange moment in old Israel after the temple had been completed. Trumpeters and singers were in the middle of praising and playing when a thick cloud fell and they were unable to proceed.

'It's all right,' Solomon told them, 'the Lord said that he would dwell in the dark cloud.'

Secondly, as we read this passage we recall that we are guardians of the mystical, spiritually practical truth that where there is a crucifixion there can be a resurrection. These verses are about pain and rejection and mockery. They are pregnant with waste and disappointment and despair.

They were a prelude to the greatest triumph in the history of the universe.

The dust may never really settle for the people in those American cities, but the Lord does dwell in the cloud. Like those brave fire-fighters in the city of New York who simply would *not* give up, he will take the hand of anyone who is lost in the darkness – any kind of darkness. He has been doing it for two thousand years.

His disaster became our salvation.

89

The Death of Jesus

15 : 33 – 41

When it was noon, darkness came over the whole land until three in the afternoon.

At three o'clock Jesus cried out with a loud voice, 'Eloi, Eloi, lema sabachthani?' which means, 'My God, my God, why have you forsaken me?'

When some of the bystanders heard it, they said, 'Listen, he is calling for Elijah.'

And someone ran, filled a sponge with sour wine, put it on a stick, and gave it to him to drink, saying, 'Wait, let us see whether Elijah will come to take him down.'

Then Jesus gave a loud cry and breathed his last. And the curtain of the temple was torn in two, from top to bottom. Now when the centurion, who stood facing him, saw that in this way he breathed his last, he said, 'Truly this man was God's Son!'

There were also women looking on from a distance; among them were Mary Magdalene, and Mary the mother of James the younger and of Joses, and Salome. These used to follow him and provided for him when he was in Galilee; and there were many other women who had come up with him to Jerusalem.

HERE ARE THREE THINGS THAT ARE TOO IMPORTANT NOT TO mention.

The first is that anguished cry of desolation from the heart of a son who had trusted his father and now, in the midst of pain and separation, felt deserted and betrayed. People have tried to deal with this uncomfortable phenomenon in a number of ways over the years. One theory is that Jesus was simply repeating the words of Psalm twenty-two in order to fulfil scripture. In other words, he didn't really mean it, but it had to be said to keep everything shipshape. If you like, a loose end that needed tying. The immediate reply to this theory is, of course, that scripture is never fulfilled merely when words are spoken. Scripture is fulfilled when the content and implication of those words is lived out in genuine human experience. I simply cannot imagine the Jesus I have met in this gospel mouthing verses he didn't mean in order to satisfy the demands of some item of divine bureaucracy.

No, he said it and he meant it, and we lose a marvellous gift from God if we do not accept that fact. Through this anguished cry we are allowed to know of the nearest point that the Son of God came to doubt and despair and failure in his mission to save the souls of men and women. Value it. It is for us. We know, when we cry out in exactly the same way, that Jesus was there first and that he understands.

This is sacred ground, but we stand safely on it with him.

The second thing is about the centurion. Having struggled to rid our memories of the sound of John Wayne's voice delivering this line as though he had just recognised an old acquaintance at the other side of the saloon in Dodge City, it is worth reflecting on the bare fact that this Roman soldier suddenly, spontaneously knew the true identity of the man he had just helped to crucify. What a revelation! He was the first of many, and there will be many more.

The third point concerns the women mentioned in this passage. There is a commonly held view of Jesus as a man who tended to walk about on his own or with his twelve disciples, somehow managing to survive by picking the odd ear of corn or frying the occasional fish caught by one of his piscatorially accomplished friends. A man who knew little of care or comfort. We have seen already, though, that, in his own way, Jesus was something of a networker. He made a lot of friends as well as a large number of enemies, and some of these friends will have offered physical support. Jesus certainly did not need material comforts, but nor did he embrace discomfort for its own sake, as a number of his followers have tried to do over the years. I don't know what you think, but I really love the fact that there were all these women who had made it their responsibility to offer a little tender loving care to their master when he was in Galilee and since he had come up to Jerusalem.

By and large, I would say that something very similar continues to happen today.

90

The Burial of Jesus

15 : 42 – 47

When evening had come, and since it was the day of Preparation, that is, the day before the Sabbath, Joseph of Arimathea, a respected member of the council, who was also himself waiting expectantly for the kingdom of God, went boldly to Pilate and asked for the body of Jesus. Then Pilate wondered if he were already dead; and summoning the centurion, he asked him whether he had been dead for some time. When he learned from the centurion that he was dead, he granted the body to Joseph. Then Joseph bought a linen cloth, and taking down the body, wrapped it in the linen cloth, and laid it in a tomb that had been hewn out of the rock. He then rolled a stone against the door of the tomb. Mary Magdalene and Mary the mother of Joses saw where the body was laid.

I WAS BROUGHT UP FOR THE FIRST TWELVE OR THIRTEEN YEARS of my life in the Roman Catholic church. My mother was a protestant, but my father's first wife had been a Catholic as well, so there was a sort of RC miscellanea distributed in odd corners around the house. There were leather missals, little sacred medals with images of the saints on them and, distinctly worrying for the kind of small child that I was, coloured pic-

224

tures of Jesus, looking like a benevolent Swedish hippy, but with his enlarged, bleeding heart exposed, dripping blood down the front of his robe. It puzzled me that he looked so well and unconcerned in these appalling circumstances.

I was too young to take communion at the local Roman Catholic chapel, but I had been told that when the grown-ups went up to kneel down and receive the bread and wine from the priest, these elements actually turned into the real body and blood of Jesus as they descended to the stomach. Another strange thing I learned was that there were relics – preserved parts of the bodies of important, saintly people, perhaps even Jesus himself – stored in holy places all over the world, and that these bits and pieces could sometimes have a power all of their own in the present day. There was more than a whiff of the charnel-house about all this. I was repelled, but I was also fascinated, and I did manage to grasp one facet of the truth that seemed vitally important then, and is perhaps even more important now. It is something about understanding that the physical, touchable, measureable, original body and blood of Jesus are cosmically, eternally important in the spiritual scheme of things. I no longer believe that the bread and wine of communion turn to flesh and blood as they enter my system, but I do know in the very heart of myself that the risen Jesus is not a metaphor, he is a man, who, if he wished, could still come back to earth, stroll along the banks of Galilee and cook fish for his friends – if he could find some. This is mystery to the power of a million, but it is not a barren mystery. I described in another section how much communion means to me. Every time I take the bread and wine there is a rebirth of hope. I pray that the same is true for you.

I suppose this line of thinking was initiated by the idea of Joseph of Arimathea actually coming to grips with the dead body of Jesus. The dormant, long-ago, small almost-Roman Catholic in me suddenly gasped at the idea of this man Joseph having the ultimate relic, the actual body of Jesus, placed into his arms. It was the communion of communions, the body and the blood of Jesus literally given to him, and also for him, and for you, and for me. Three days later the Son of God would rise again from the tomb, just as, when we faithfully receive into ourselves those symbols of bread and wine, he rises in us.

91

The Resurrection of Jesus

16 : 1 – 8

When the Sabbath was over, Mary Magdalene, and Mary the mother of James, and Salome bought spices, so that they might go and anoint him. And very early on the first day of the week, when the sun had risen, they went to the tomb.

They had been saying to one another, 'Who will roll away the stone for us from the entrance to the tomb?'

When they looked up, they saw that the stone, which was very large, had already been rolled back. As they entered the tomb, they saw a young man, dressed in a white robe, sitting on the right side; and they were alarmed.

But he said to them, 'Do not be alarmed; you are looking for Jesus of Nazareth, who was crucified. He has been raised; he is not here. Look, there is the place they laid him. But go, tell his disciples and Peter that he is going ahead of you to Galilee; there you will see him, just as he told you.'

So they went out and fled from the tomb, for terror and amazement had seized them; and they said nothing to anyone, for they were afraid.

AS WE GET OLDER OUR BODIES GO THROUGH MANY CHANGES. Most of these changes seem to involve either tightening or sagging. Horrible idea, isn't it? Muscles get stiff and take longer to get moving in the morning or after long periods of inactivity, while other parts of the body lose their elasticity and, for want of a better word, begin to 'droop'. I suppose I am just entering the tightening and sagging phase, but I am interested to note that, running parallel with these physical changes, there are similar psychological and emotional alterations happening as well. In my case, one of the tightenings in this area is a much greater tendency to suffer from claustrophobia, or at least, in deference to those who are chronic victims of this affliction, from claustrophobic feelings.

When I was young I don't think I cared how small a space I squeezed my body into for a game of Hide and Seek or Sardines, and as a teenager I was more than happy to cram myself into the back of a two-door car with three or four others if it meant getting a ride to a pub or a party. Of late, however, I find myself experiencing something approaching breathless panic at the very idea of being confined in a tiny space with no means of getting out. I think it was a ride in one of those two-door vehicles that first alerted me to this change. I was squashed into the rear seat of a tiny car, with the large and looming back of a fellow-traveller in front of me, creating an impassable barrier to the door beside the front passenger seat. Lurid pictures started to fill my mind.

We would crash and the car would catch fire. I would be sandwiched between pieces of twisted metal in a burning hulk, unable even to attempt to move or escape because the lifeless or unconscious bulk of my fellow-passenger was blocking the way. I could feel myself beginning to sweat and breathe heavily as these awful images gripped my imagination.

Somehow I survived that trip without demanding that the driver should stop and release me so that I could stretch and breathe and insist on moving to the front, but I knew then and I know now that I shall never willingly travel in such a situation again. Fortunately I am more than averagely tall and broad, so I am almost always offered the front seat anyway. I make it a point to graciously accept.

The same thing has started to happen in lifts. I was in one the other day in a hotel in Holland, a very small lift, about the size of a large coffin. It stopped halfway between two floors and the light went out. For one awful moment I thought I was going to start shouting and screaming and kicking against the walls and the door, but then it started moving again and the light came back on. A few moments later I staggered into my room and collapsed on the bed. For the rest of my stay I walked up and down the stairs.

I am telling you all this because it might help to explain why the resurrection of Jesus is a matter of such importance and joy for me. As I approach my mid-fifties, and the triplet spectres of old-age, disablement and death keep poking their heads up to grin at me from unexpected corners like targets in a shooting gallery, I rejoice that I am not trapped within the cramped confines of a cycle that begins with birth and ends with death and oblivion or separation from God. I know that I would feel that same breathless panic in my heart as I felt in the car or the lift, if I truly believed that the whole complex, beautiful, tragic thing ends in dumbness or darkness.

Jesus has risen. It is finished. The Son of God has done the thing that sets us free from a doom-laden destiny and allows us to go home. There will continue to be life, love, laughter, a meeting of the eyes and the sweet, sweet taste of sparkling spring mornings. There will be not a hint of religion, nor a trace of narrowness, and as C. S. Lewis says, there will be lots of surprises.

Listen, I really cannot pretend to fully understand redemption or atonement, but I can tell you that I believe in them. I believe in him. I believe in Jesus. The voice of the Servant King is as strong and reassuring and authoritative now as it was two thousand years ago, as recorded in the gospel of John:

'I have told you these things, so that in me you may have peace. In this world you will have trouble. But take heart! I have overcome the world.'

92

An Abrupt Ending?

16 : 9 – 10

And all that had been commanded them they told briefly to those around Peter. And afterward Jesus himself sent out through them, from east to west, the sacred and imperishable proclamation of eternal salvation.

IT IS A BIT OF AN ABRUPT ENDING ISN'T IT? THIS IS ONE OF two alternative conclusions for the gospel of Mark. The other one is much longer and, I gather, was written by someone else at a later date. I'm quite glad, really, because it has a little too much of a 'Tabloid' feeling about it for my taste. No, this one will do for now, although I do warmly recommend that you read the endings of the other gospels. There is much to enjoy and learn in the record of those strange and momentous days following the resurrection, especially in the gospels of Luke and John.

In one sense, though, this brief ending does say the most important thing of all. The commission of Jesus to his disciples is for us as well as for them. The message of everlasting life is from God, and it can never be destroyed. Our task is to make sure that as many people as possible are given the chance to hear, understand and act on this information. We may feel inadequate and unsure about our role in all this, but look again at the words in this passage. The courageous, uncompromising, compassionate, smiling, authoritative Jesus whom we have met in these pages will send the message out through us. If we can *truly* believe that, it will help us to be brave and determined and obedient.

May God bless you and me in our walk with Jesus.

Silver Birches

A Novel

Adrian Plass, Internationally Bestselling Author

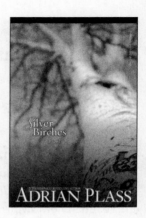

When David Herrick receives an invitation to a reunion from a long-forgotten acquaintance, his first reaction is to refuse. He isn't feeling very sociable since his wife, Jessica, died six months ago.

But the invitation comes from Angela, one of his wife's oldest friends — and mysteriously, she has something for him from his beloved Jessica. Reluctant but curious, he visits Headly Manor.

When the friends gather, they no longer resemble the fresh-faced group of twenty years ago. One has been deserted by her husband, another has lost his faith, and another is filled with anger and bitterness. As they have less than forty-eight hours with each other, they decide to be vulnerable and bear their souls.

This poignant and moving story blends Adrian Plass's rich style of writing with his knack for addressing the deep issues we all face, such as faith, grief, love ... and fear.

Softcover: 978-0-310-29203-6

Pick up a copy today at your favourite bookstore!

The Sacred Diary of Adrian Plass, Aged 37 ¾

Adrian Plass

Saturday, December 14th

Feel led to keep a diary. A sort of spiritual log for the benefit of others in the future. Each new divine insight and experience will shine like a beacon in the darkness!

Can't think of anything to put in today.

Still, tomorrow's Sunday. Must be something on a Sunday, surely?

* * *

Adrian Plass is hilarious, pure and simple. His readers are legion – and this is the bestselling book that started it all, converting thousands of people who love to laugh into avid Plass readers.

The Sacred Diary of Adrian Plass, Aged 37¾, is merriment and facetiousness at its best – a journal of the wacky Christian life of Plass's fictional alter ego, who chronicles in his 'sacred' diary the daily goings-on in the lives of ordinary-but-somewhat-eccentric people he knows and meets. Reading it will doeth good like a medicine!

Softcover: 978-0-310-26912-0

Pick up a copy today at your favourite bookstore!

ZONDERVAN®
.com

The Sacred Diary of Adrian Plass, Christian, Aged 45 ¾

Adrian Plass

Adrian Plass lovers got their initial baptism of laughter through his bestseller *The Sacred Diary of Adrian Plass, Aged 37 ¾*. The author's account of 'serious spiritual experiences' naturally made him in demand as a public speaker – so of course another diary was inevitable.

The Sacred Diary of Adrian Plass, Christian Speaker, Aged 45 ¾ continues the misadventures of Adrian's fictional alter ego. As Plass gathers regularly with his support group, we meet old friends, including his longsuffering wife, Anne; son, Gerald, now grown but no less irrepressible; loony and lovable Leonard Thynn; Edwin, the wise church elder; and Richard and Doreen Cook, who are just as religious as ever. We also meet some new characters, such as Stephanie Widgeon, who only seems to have one thing to say, ever ... and who knows, we might even find out why Leonard Thynn borrowed Adrian's cat all those years ago.

And finally – what is a banner ripping seminar?

Softcover: 978-0-310-26913-7

Pick up a copy today at your favourite bookstore!

Share Your Thoughts

With the Author: Your comments will be forwarded to the author when you send them to *zauthor@zondervan.com*.

With Zondervan: Submit your review of this book by writing to *zreview@zondervan.com*.

Free Online Resources at
www.zondervan.com

Zondervan AuthorTracker: Be notified whenever your favourite authors publish new books, go on tour, or post an update about what's happening in their lives at www.zondervan.com/authortracker.

Daily Bible Verses and Devotions: Enrich your life with daily Bible verses or devotions that help you start every morning focused on God. Visit www.zondervan.com/newsletters.

Free Email Publications: Sign up for newsletters on Christian living, academic resources, church ministry, fiction, children's resources, and more. Visit www.zondervan.com/newsletters.

Zondervan Bible Search: Find and compare Bible passages in a variety of translations at www.zondervanbiblesearch.com.

Other Benefits: Register yourself to receive online benefits like coupons and special offers, or to participate in research.

ZONDERVAN®

ZONDERVAN.com/
AUTHORTRACKER
follow your favorite authors